FIGURE SKATING
with CARLO FASSI

FIGURE

with Gregory Smith
Editorial consultant, Nina Stark

illustrated by WALT SPITZMILLER

SKATING
with CARLO FASSI

CHARLES SCRIBNER'S SONS   NEW YORK

To my mother

A skater and a mother
but never a skating mother!

Library of Congress Cataloging in Publication Data

Fassi, Carlo.
  Figure skating with Carlo Fassi.

   1. Skating.   I. Smith, Gregory, 1953-   joint
author.   II. Stark, Nina.   III. Title.
GV849.F3   796.91   80-18013
ISBN 0-684-16314-4

ACKNOWLEDGMENTS

To Dick Button I am sincerely grateful for suggesting my name to Charles Scribner's Sons.

My special thanks go to Walt Spitzmiller for his superb drawings and for the opportunity to collaborate on this book; to Gregory Smith for the not-so-easy task of understanding and transcribing my English tapes; to my former pupil and skating professional Nina Stark, whose suggestions and critical comments I greatly appreciate; and, at Scribners, to editors Wendy Rieder and Patricia Gallagher for their thoughtful guidance.

I wish to acknowledge the skaters who spent many hours on the ice for the photo sessions: Robin Cousins, Scott Cramer, Susan Dirano, Jackie Farrell, Lorenzo Fassi, Dana Graham, Simone Grigorescu, Scott Hamilton, Yuri Ohata, Alicia Risberg, Jill Sawyer, Jill Spitzmiller, Emi Watanabe, and Brenda Welliver.

Many thanks to Dr. Hugh Graham for his comments on nutrition.

To my wife, Christa, I am indebted for her help, suggestions, corrections, and encouragement.

And, finally, I want to express my gratitude to all my students from 1954 to today: I hope they learned from me as much as I learned from them. Without them, this book would not exist.

CONTENTS

FOREWORD
by Dick Button

The first time I saw Carlo Fassi he was roaring down the rink with arms, legs, and snow flying in all directions. The year was 1948 and Carlo was representing Italy in the Olympic Games in St. Moritz. He had flare, talent, excitement, and fun. Since then we have skated in competition against each other many times. I have watched with interest and enthusiasm his progress as a teacher, producer, international politician, husband, father, counselor, and guide in all aspects of the fine art of figure skating.

Carlo has been an influence in skating for more than thirty years. With the support of his beautiful wife Christa, he successfully guided the competitive careers of such skating greats as Peggy Fleming, John Curry, Dorothy Hamill, and Robin Cousins. He's been in so many places at the same time that I have a suspicion there are really two Carlo Fassis. Carlo is the perfect one to arrange his thoughts in a book of this nature. He's at the top of his career as a teacher and coach. I consider him one of my most entertaining friends and I know his career will continue to grow in triple and quadruple leaps.

Dick Button

New York City

PREFACE

I wrote this book for both the beginner and the more advanced skater. With Walt Spitzmiller's superb drawings, skaters can visualize the figures, jumps, and spins and, with the directions and tips I give, master them.

Beginning with taking the first step onto the ice to performing the double Axel, the skater in each drawing is at the level of achievement of the element that is presented. The positions of the skaters in the drawings—especially the beginning elements—are realistic; that is, they are good, but not perfect! This is to give the reader an accurate idea how skaters usually look during the various stages of development.

The techniques I describe are the ones that have helped me through twenty-five years of teaching. I don't claim they are the only ones. I believe that a good teacher has to adjust his or her technique to the ability and personality of each skater. I believe that what we call the style of the skater is always an indescribable combination of body structure and personality, as well as mastery of skating elements.

SKATES, LESSONS, and TRAINING

Skating is both a sport and a form of artistic expression that can be learned and enjoyed by people of all ages. Whether intending to compete or skate purely for recreation, all beginners tend to ask the same questions before stepping onto the ice for the first time. In this chapter, I share with you answers and advice I have given about equipment, lessons, and training during more than twenty years of coaching.

FIGURE SKATES

There is no more important piece of equipment than a properly fitted skate. The boot must be the proper size, the laces must be tied correctly, and the blade must be in the correct position. If any one of these is not perfect, your skating will be adversely affected.

Blades

The figure skate has a high boot made of fine leather that is attached to a steel blade, easily recognized by the "teeth" near the toe, called toe picks or toe rakes. These toe picks are used primarily for specific jumps and spins. The blade is not flat, as it may at first appear, but gently curved. The curve in the blade means that only a small portion of the blade touches the ice at any one time. The less of the blade that makes contact with the ice, the easier it is for a skater to turn and execute certain moves.

The figure blade is grooved lengthwise, giving it two distinct edges—an inside edge and an outside one. If the skater stands straight so that both edges of each blade are on the ice, movement will be straight forward or backward. Each blade will leave a marking of two parallel lines, or traces, on the ice. If the skater leans left or right, however, only one edge of each skate will touch the ice and the skater will curve in the direction of the lean. The "edged blade" makes it easy for a skater to turn by simply changing his or her weight over the blades.

The figure blade is about one-eighth of an inch thick and runs the length of the boot. The entire blade consists of a flat steel plate supported by short steel posts, called stanchions. The stanchions are short to keep the skater's body low, or close to the ice, as a lower center of gravity gives the skater better control over his or her movements. The stanchions on hockey skates are taller, as the movement required is different from that in figure skating. It is best that a beginner start with figure skates, regardless of ultimate skating goals. In fact, most of the best professional hockey players have had figure-skating lessons to make them better skaters.

Advanced figure skaters require more specific refinements in their skates. For instance, the blades for the spectacular jumps and spins of free skating have larger toe picks angled closer to the ice than those blades designed for figures. The free-skating blade also has a deeper groove between the edges than does a normal blade, causing the blade to cut deeper into the ice, providing more stability in landing from jumps.

The blade used for compulsory, or "school," figures has a greater lengthwise curve than beginners' blades, as well as an exceptionally shallow hollow between the edges. The curve of the blade makes turning very easy for the skater who is performing the intricate and delicate compulsory figures. The blades also glide across the ice better than other blades, leaving a clear, clean trace. The first toe pick on blades for compulsory figures has been removed for better rocking motion without interference from the pick. Advanced competitive skaters usually have two sets of blades and boots—one for figures and one for free skating.

Most top-level ice dancers use thinner, flatter blades than those used by singles skaters. The thin, flat blades help them attain and hold great speed and stability by creating less friction with the ice and gripping the ice well, to make strong, powerful strokes. The toe picks of these blades are set higher off the ice than those on normal blades. Higher toe picks reduce the possibility of tripping, since the dancers perform complex footwork very close together. To further reduce the risk of accident, the heels of the blades are cut short so that partners will not spike each other as they skate close together.

Boots

All figure-skate boots have heels, long tongues, and tops that usually taper upward in front. The heels of adult-size skates are about two inches high.

The skating boot is perhaps the most crucial element in a skater's per-

THE FIGURE SKATE

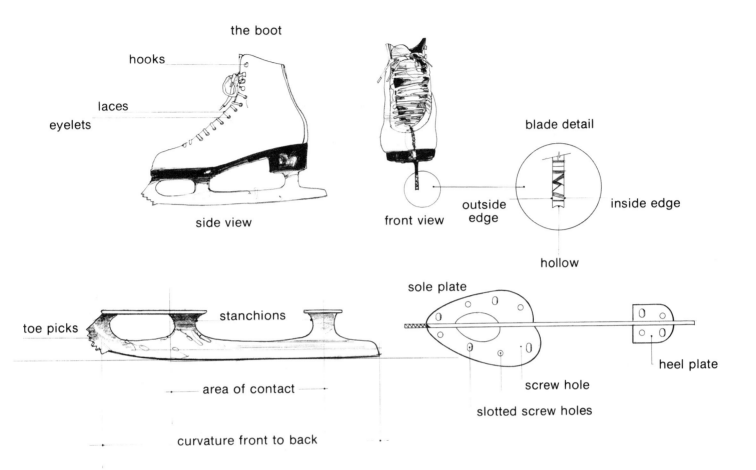

the boot

hooks

laces

eyelets

side view

front view

blade detail

outside edge

inside edge

hollow

sole plate

toe picks

stanchions

area of contact

curvature front to back

screw hole

slotted screw holes

heel plate

formance. A boot that is not correctly fitted can cause all sorts of problems. Many champion skaters have stories to tell of foot problems caused by ill-fitting boots worn early in their careers. Skating boots should be smaller than the skater's normal shoe. If this sounds odd, remember, these boots are made for skating, not for walking; they should "fit like a glove." Wear only a thin pair of cotton socks or tights with skates; thick wool socks can cause perspiration and actually make your feet colder as the perspiration freezes.

The figure-skating boot must fit snugly so that when the boot is laced the heel will not budge and the instep is held firmly in place. Boots of good quality have built-in leather or steel arch supports, or counters, to help hold the foot properly. When trying on skate boots, do not confuse comfort with correct fit. The steel-reinforced insteps are made to prevent the ankles from giving way under the force of the body weight while landing from a jump. Toes are the only part of the feet that require a little room. Toes must be able to move a bit up and down and sideways, to help control balance.

Where the boot curves to the shape of the foot eyelets guide the laces; as the boot conforms to the shape of the leg, hooks are used instead of eyelets.

The tongue of the boot is wide and thickly padded. The padding makes the boot more comfortable when it is laced. The tongue is designed to curve around the sides of the ankle when laced and to allow the boot to adapt to body movements.

New boots must, of course, be "broken in." A good way to do this, although it may seem strange to a beginner, is to wet your bare feet and then place them in the boots. This moistens the soft leather lining in the boots, causing the damp leather to conform to the shape of the foot. As the leather dries, it molds itself to the exact shape of the foot and shrinks slightly.

Before attaching the blades, it is important to preserve the soles and heels of the boots with a waterproofing agent made for skating boots, available at most skate shops and leather goods stores.

Attaching the Blades

After the boots are waterproofed, the blades are screwed into the boots. The blades first must be positioned correctly—they are to be screwed to the sole just inside the center line that divides the boot in half lengthwise. In this critical placement the skater's weight is more effectively distributed over the blades, eliminating any tendency of the ankles to collapse inward.

At first only two temporary screws are used to attach the blades—one in the heel and one under the ball of the foot. As the skater walks in the newly attached skates, the fitter can determine if the weight is distributed properly through the foot. If not, adjustments are made. An experienced skater can in time feel any need for adjustment. If all is well, permanent screws are added to hold the blade firmly to the boot. However, even when the blade is perfectly positioned, not all the screw slots in the steel plate of the blade are used. This way, a loose blade can be tightened and any future adjustments can be made more easily.

Lacing the Boots

Perfectly fitting boots with a perfectly attached blade now must be laced correctly, or the best boot and blade won't perform as they were designed to. Laces tied too loosely across the instep take vital support away from the ankle; laces tied too tightly at the top impair the normal circulation of blood to the foot.

When the boots are laced, the toes must be able to move up, down, and sideways while the tension of the laces is snug at the instep. Lace the rest of the boot just tight enough so a finger can slip inside the back of the boot. This room allows the leg to bend without decreasing support for the ankle. However, in order to separate the tighter tension of the bottom lacing from the looser lacing needed at the top, the laces are crossed and tied at the ankle after the first hook.

When the boot is laced so the toes can still move and blood can still flow through the foot, tie the knot at the top of the boot. Wrap any leftover lace around the leg, then tie another knot, tucking the remaining lace firmly inside the boot. Never let laces dangle; if they come untied, retie them immediately. Countless accidents have occurred from laces coming undone, tripping unsuspecting skaters. Tying secure knots is the best way to avoid these accidents. Also be sure the laces are neither frayed nor about to break, and replace them at the first sign of wear.

Renting versus Buying Skates

Proper equipment is essential for the full enjoyment of any sport. Nowhere is this more true than in figure skating. The best way to guarantee improvement in performance, as well as to increase safety, is to have your own equipment and maintain it carefully.

Most public ice-skating rinks offer skates for rent. Initially, a skater may borrow or rent skates to see if the sport will hold his or her interest. But the beginner will find that rented skates are, more often than not, broken-down specimens that have been abused by scores of feet and offer little or no support. Active interest in skating requires, above all else, an investment in skates.

When buying skates, go to a specialist, usually found in rink or pro skate shops. Avoid the sometimes attractive department stores, whose staff is likely to have little knowledge of the importance of properly fitting skates. For children, however, a good place to buy skates is often the second-hand shop at an ice rink or figure-skating club. These skates are usually satisfactory for rapidly growing feet. Some shops and clubs also offer a reasonable trade-in for skates that have been kept in good condition.

The serious skaters invariably buy their boots and blades separately and have them fitted together to each foot's specification. Boots and blades riveted together "at the factory" may be suitable for the occasional skater but not for the serious student. Blades that must be attached to the boot allow the skater to adjust the placement of the blades to suit his or her body and to realign them later if required. Also, boots and blades purchased separately tend to be superior in material and workmanship to skates bought as a unit.

Skate blades are made of high-quality steel, hard and strong enough to hold its sharpness (its edge) for some time. The length of time a blade will stay sharp depends, of course, on the frequency with which the skate is used and the quality of the steel.

As a rule, the smoother the weld between the blade and the stanchion plate, the better the steel, as better steel generally makes a smoother weld. The highest priced, top-quality blades are designed for advanced skaters and are not intended for the beginning skater, but be sure to get the best quality for your own needs.

SKATE CARE

Skates, like all instruments, need care. Properly maintained skates not only last longer but also look better. It is easy to care for your skates and requires very little time, but to be effective, skate care must become part of your daily skating regimen.

Boots

Moisture from the ice, the changes of temperature between the home and rink and ice surface, and even perspiration that penetrates the fine leather of the boot all dilute the natural oils in the leather, causing it to become brittle and eventually to crack.

Even with waterproofed boots, a regular treatment with saddle soap (a pastelike wax available at any good shoe store) will prevent any moisture from seeping into and attacking the leather. Skaters who practice daily should apply saddle soap to their boots once every six weeks, whereas the average skater should apply it at least every six months.

Keeping white boots white is a perpetual problem. The best polishes are the creams that come in tins and are applied with a brush or cloth. Liquids with their own applicators are more of a cover than a polish, and although they are more convenient and require less elbow grease, they do not provide the protection that pastes do. After applying polish, buff as you would any fine leather.

Once the boots are really scuffed, only the liquid polish will cover the spot. However, repeated treatment with liquid polish will eventually penetrate the leather and cause it to crack, as any liquid is an enemy of fine leather (remember the purpose of the saddle soap). Wash the laces regularly and have loose eyelets repaired or replaced by a skilled craftsman at a rink or skate shop.

Blades

As you skate, the blades naturally become cold and wet. After each use, wipe the blades clean of snow and moisture with a lint-free cloth. Some believe a chamois cloth is best, while others argue that an ordinary washcloth is just as good: actually, both work well. After they are wiped clean, allow the skates to warm up to room temperature. Let them warm by themselves—*never put the cold blades near a radiator, as this sudden change in temperature could distort their shape.*

Moisture will form on the blades (through condensation), so wipe them dry again. If you are going to put the skates away for a long period of time, you should first rub the blades lightly with petroleum jelly (Vaseline).

Skate Guards

Watch top-class skaters—they never step off the ice without first wiping the snow from their blades with their fingers and covering the blades with skate guards. Skate guards cover the length of the blade, including the toe picks; they are inexpensive and are usually made of rubber, plastic, or wood. I find that rubber guards are the best.

Even though they are of high-quality steel, blades can be easily damaged and must be protected by skate guards when off the ice. Almost all ice rinks today are surrounded by a carpet or rubber matting, but the sophisticated edges of the blades need to be protected from the dirt and grit that always accumulates on the mat, regardless of how clean it appears. Never walk in skates without guards on concrete, tile, or wood, as that will certainly dull or nick the edges of the blades permanently. A good rule to remember is never to walk anywhere without skate guards. Once you have removed the skates, take off the guards and turn the guards upside down to dry. From your pro shop buy blade covers, which are made of wool or cloth. They will keep the blades dry until you skate again. Do not store skates with guards on, because the blades will rust as the guards never completely dry out.

A good habit to acquire is to put the skate guards in a specific place each time you step on the ice. This way, you always know where the guards are and they are readily available as you step off the ice. You can then put them on without missing a step. Most skaters have had the surprise of a sudden fall when they step on the ice with their guards still on. It is an experience not easily forgotten, since the suddenness of the fall makes it all that much harder. In fact, many famous skaters have appeared before audiences by flying across the ice in the most graceless position, only because their skate guards were still protecting their blades.

Sharpening

Although skate guards protect blades from damage, they cannot prevent the edges of the blade from losing their sharpness. The length of time a blade will keep its edge depends on many things. How often the blade is used and how it is used, the quality of the steel in the blade, the depth of the hollow between the edges, the temperature and resulting hardness of the ice, the purity and degree of roughness of the ice itself, and the weight of the skater all determine how long the blades will hold their edges.

In the beginning, an instructor can judge if blades need sharpening, or "grinding," by running a finger along the edges. In time, through experience, you will be able to determine when your skates need sharpening. Skates used every day may need sharpening every few weeks, though skates used only occasionally may hold their edges for two years.

Today almost all rinks have a craftsman who specializes in the complex art of sharpening or grinding blades. But there are countless horror stories of work done by incompetent or inexperienced sharpeners. Skate-sharpening horrors take many forms. A careless sharpener may eliminate the bottom toe pick, or may put a nick or, worse, a gash into the edges. One edge may be ground shorter than the other, or the hollow between the edges may be so deep that the skater can hardly move on the ice because the blades bite so deeply into the ice. On the other hand, if the hollow is too shallow, the skater cannot grip the ice at all and will skid haphazardly about. An incompetent workman has also been known to remove the back of the heel, or make the radius of the blade—its curve—so large that turning is almost impossible. Finally, an overzealous sharpener may grind away so much steel that one skate is lower than the other.

A competitor should sharpen his or her blades no less than every four weeks for free skating and every three to four weeks for figures. You need an especially smooth edge for skating figures as a flat, dull edge will slow down the execution of the figure. Blades must be extremely well sharpened for a competition, but have it done a full three days before. This allows you a few sessions on the ice to become accustomed to the newly treated edges.

Sharpening is very, very important. I would love to see skaters learn how to maintain the edge temporarily themselves by "stoning" their own blades, especially if they enter international competition, as they may not always be able to find someone who can sharpen to their satisfaction. With a hand sharpening stone, a skater can shave from the edges (without affecting the hollow of the blade) nicks and rough burrs that hamper the smooth flow of the blade.

The last thing I want to say about equipment care is this: every good figure skater (and by this I mean the competitor who is beyond the third test) should replace skates every eight or nine months. It may seem excessive, but when you consider how much lessons cost and how much time and energy are devoted to practicing, you will see that it is very foolish not to always have the best equipment.

THE SKATER'S CLOTHING

Clothing for skating should be functional, sturdy, and warm, offering some protection in case of falls, but it should also be attractive, close-fitting, light (but not bulky), and allow for maximum movement.

Boys should wear slacks with sweaters or light jackets over sweaters. Parkas and long scarves should not be worn. Girls should wear a pleated skating skirt or a tightly fitted one-piece dress with matching panties. Tights and leotards should be worn not only for warmth but also for protection. Gloves and perhaps a cap are recommended. If the temperature is very cold, disregard appearance and wear warm but suitable clothing.

Men should wear fitted slacks and a sweater. Sometimes a jacket and tie are appropriate, especially for dance sessions at a skating club. Dark colors are common.

Women usually wear a short skirt with a blouse, sweater, or jacket. One-piece skating dresses with matching panties and tights are popular, as are the Polar one-piece warmup suits for both men and women.

If your feet get cold, invest in a pair of boot covers that fit over the boots. Do not wear wool socks; they disturb the fit of your boot and may also cause perspiration, making your feet colder as the perspiration freezes.

TRAINING

Lessons

I am frequently asked by parents at what age they should introduce skating to their children. The right time for a child to start skating is the subject of much debate. As in all sports, competitive figure skaters seem to be getting younger and younger each year. Children sometimes start their skating lessons even before they enter school. The age at which lessons should begin is different for boys and girls because they grow at different rates; girls are generally ready for skating one or two years earlier. If they are to have a serious skating career, girls should begin skating when they are four years old, and no later than age seven. Boys should begin when they are six years old, but no later than age eight.

The next question parents generally ask is "How should I introduce my child to skating?" First of all, don't invest a lot of money in new skates and private lessons initially. (This applies to beginners of all ages.) I am definitely in favor of renting skates in the beginning to see if skating is of interest to your child. Just make sure the skates are in good condition and fit snugly. If the leather in the boot is not firm or the blades are dull and rusty, ask for another pair. You will rarely find a perfect pair of rental skates, but I still believe you should rent rather than buy for the first few trips to the rink. When you see that your child is interested in skating and likes it, then you should buy a good pair of skates from a pro shop.

As far as the first pair of skates for children is concerned, I am really against double runners—those beginner skates that resemble a tiny sled attached to each foot. It may be easier for a small child to stand up on the ice with double runners, but they neither glide as normal skates do nor teach anything about the actual process of skating.

Young children have no fear of falling and often seem to delight in it. Their bodies are near the ice and they are so relaxed when they fall that they bounce right back up again. As children rarely are injured from the spills they take when learning to skate, I recommend that they start out on real figure skates.

After investing in a good pair of skates, the beginner should take group lessons at a public rink or skating club to learn the very basic skating techniques. After a few lessons young children should be allowed to skate in public sessions and play around with other young skaters. One of the problems coaches face with some advanced skaters is that while they know all the right techniques, they appear somewhat awkward on the ice. Skating doesn't seem to be second nature to them. This is because, as young children, they started taking serious lessons before they really had a feel for the ice. So, for the first few months, encourage your child to skate around the rink, playing tag and other games to really enjoy just plain skating. Private lessons should not start until the child displays a genuine interest, demonstrates natural ability, and really enjoys the sport.

Finding a Good Coach

How can one find and evaluate a good coach? That is a tough question. Effective coaching is always a result of the relationship between the pro and the pupil. First of all, the professional has to like students—especially very young students—and he or she must be patient. Sometimes excellent pros are not good coaches because they are too demanding and want to obtain results too quickly from a little skater.

One serious mistake in teaching young skaters is to introduce highly technical terms and explanations. The child of six, seven, or eight will not understand and may even lose interest in skating.

Second, the pro should be able to explain what he or she is trying to teach the pupil in the simplest possible terms. One element should be introduced at a time. I view coaching as a slow process that allows the student to assimilate and perfect one step before moving on to another.

Finally, in evaluating a coach, an important trait to consider is whether he or she makes skating enjoyable for the student. The professional who is positive and encouraging can expect students to adopt the same attitude about their skating and make steady progress through self-confidence and love of the sport.

How Hard Should a Child Be Pushed?

I believe that until around the age of twelve most children are not competent to make major decisions on their own. I think that if children have natural ability and enjoy skating, their parents should decide whether this potential should be developed, and enforce their decision. There will be days when young skaters are very enthusiastic and will skate for hours without stopping, offset by days when they want nothing to do with the sport. It is on those days that parents should step in and say firmly: "You have embarked on a possible skating career; you have talent; it has cost us a lot of money, and we feel you should continue." Children should not be terrorized, but they should understand (and will eventually appreciate) their parents' commitment on their behalf. Peggy Fleming would never have become a world champion without the strong but loving encouragement of her mother.

What It Takes
to Become a Serious Competitor

In addition to natural ability, interest, and firm parents, it takes practice. An eight- to ten-year-old novice who is on the first to third test needs a *minimum* of two hours a day on figures and one hour a day on free skating. This is every day for twelve months of the year with two vacations—like two weeks in September and two weeks in March.

I think that four to six lessons a week are plenty—divided equally between figure and free skating, and supplemented by classes in ballet or modern dance at least twice a week. Many of my colleagues hold different opinions on the number of lessons needed. Some believe in two, three, and even four lessons a day. To my way of thinking, this discourages students from thinking for themselves. With this number of lessons, they will begin to think like their pros. No athlete wins Olympic medals based entirely on the coach's direction. I believe that the coach contributes only 30 percent of what it takes to become a champion. The other 70 percent is the skater's will, determination, intelligence, and ability to compete. Therefore, I encourage my pupils to think for themselves, discipline themselves, and even train themselves.

Costs

No one ever said skating is inexpensive. The minimum cost is a few thousand dollars a year, and the maximum is $10,000 to $15,000. When a top skater enters international competition, foreign travel is involved. The skater's expenses are usually paid for by the national figure-skating association, but not the coach's. I've known skaters whose parents couldn't afford to accompany them to far-off competitions, but they usually managed to find a way. Many times a sponsor turns up who will pay most, if not all, of the expenses of the skater's party.

Does Skating Interfere with School?

Most skating can, in the beginning of an amateur career, be scheduled around the normal school day. Skaters often practice for two hours in the early morning before school and then again after school or in the evening. It is interesting to note that the majority of good skaters are also good students. Skaters must learn to discipline themselves, and this extends to their schoolwork. They develop a strong sense of concentration and study their textbooks as hard as they study their figures and free skating.

As the skater improves, practice time is increased, which bites into the school routine. If the skater is efficient, both skating and school can be balanced. Giving up school to skate is a bad idea for many reasons. Skating can take the place of school, and may be considered forced, boring, and repetitive to the skater—no longer the "fun" thing to do before and after school. When skating is a recreation, skaters enjoy it more and seem to do better.

Getting to the Top

There are many individual paths leading up the competitive ladder. Some skaters, such as Dorothy Hamill, who started skating relatively late but progressed rapidly, get to the top very quickly. And not all skating depends on skill, because luck does figure in many skating careers—ask any skater. Some great skaters have difficulty performing well in front of an audience, and they have lost key competitions as a result. Other skaters do very well, and their initial success opens the door to future competitions. The real secret, however, is perseverance.

There are good judges and there are judges who you will feel are not as capable; in the long run of a career, they seem to balance out. You should never be discouraged by a judge's mark, nor should you—or your parents— ever criticize a judge. To make the most of the judges you encounter, you must emphasize what you do well and play down your lesser skills. There is no substitute, however, for competence and originality. Let the judges know what a special skater you are. Take care of your health, stay in good condition, and you will rise to the occasion for the crucial competitions.

BEGINNING TO SKATE

The first time you step onto the ice may be both exciting and a little frightening. Well, how does everyone usually start to skate?

I suggest that you step on the ice holding on to the hand of an experienced adult skater or to the barrier that surrounds the rink. Place your right hand on the barrier, extending your left arm to provide balance, and proceed along in a counterclockwise movement, as this is the direction in which most skaters travel around the rink.

Step naturally, first with the left and then with the right foot until you get accustomed to the new feeling of having two blades under your feet. Don't try to glide suddenly or do some strange things because, before you know it, you will completely lose control. Always keep your right hand on the barrier or holding on to a skater who accompanies you.

When you feel you have a little more control and no longer need the barrier for balance, then it is time to step away, bringing both arms toward the front. Now you are ready to learn figure skating.

In the following drawings, we have depicted the positions skaters are most likely to assume in any stage of development. While we describe in words the ideal position, the drawings show what really occurs in training sessions. In other words, even the serious, experienced skater doesn't always have the perfect body alignment. The models for these drawings are skaters in training sessions.

WALKING ON THE ICE

This drawing shows the front position of a small boy with his coach on the ice. As you can see, the boy's body is in an almost upright position, and his arms are stretched out slightly forward. When we were children, we all tried to balance as though we were on a tightrope, placing one foot after another. The movement I am going to describe is similar.

First, stand with both feet on the ice, your body weight distributed equally over each foot. Bend your knees slightly, keeping the upper part of your body erect. As you can see from the side view of this position in the next drawing, the boy has a tendency to bend forward. This is to be expected; as a beginner, you may be thinking it is better to fall forward than backward and you will position your body accordingly.

With knees bent, raise one foot, keeping your weight over the foot that is on the ice. With your raised foot, make a very small step, moving the entire blade forward onto the ice. Shift your weight to that foot and raise the other.

Make a series of these small steps, remembering to keep your knees bent and your weight over the foot that is on the ice. Don't try to slide at this point, just walk.

After you have done this exercise for a while, you will start to feel a sense of sliding on the ice. When this happens, you are ready to go on to *sculling*.

WALKING ON THE ICE *(continued)*

SCULLING

1

2

The easiest way to begin skating forward is to *scull*, or push your feet away from and then toward each other to generate motion. The first push to get started is relatively hard, so it helps to have someone give you a gentle nudge to get you going.

Begin sculling with both feet together, toes turned out comfortably (Position 1). Raise your arms to the sides, bend your knees slightly, and push both feet into the ice, letting the feet slide out (Position 2). When your feet are about two feet apart (Position 3), slowly turn your toes in (Position 4). Bring your feet together by pulling them in, straightening your knees at the same time. When your feet are parallel repeat the sculling motion.

3   4

Dorothy Hamill's skating career started when she asked her parents for lessons on how to skate backward the way her friends did. You can develop the ability to skate backward by taking small steps backward, in the same manner as you walked forward on the ice in the previous exercise, and by simply reversing the movements you used to scull forward. Follow the drawing for forward sculling but in reverse order. That is, start with your toes fairly close together and your heels turned out. Bend your knees and push your feet into the ice and out. When your feet are about two feet apart, turn your heels in and straighten your legs to bring your feet together before repeating the motion.

THE DIP

After you are able to glide a small distance on two skates, this short exercise will improve your balance.

While gliding on both feet, spread your arms to the sides and slowly bend your body down in a dip position, keeping your weight forward. Without stopping, raise your body to an upright position and glide for a distance, then repeat the dipping motion. After you feel comfortable performing this

Front view

up-and-down movement, try to dip down a little farther. See if you can do two or three of these at a little faster speed.

It is important to keep your ankles straight in the dip position. A bent ankle or an ankle that is turned inward will reduce your speed and impair your balance.

Side view

GLIDING ON ONE SKATE

With this exercise I am going to introduce two very basic skating terms: the *skating* side and the *free* side. In Position 1 of this drawing, the boy is *skating* on his right foot; his left foot is off the ice. Therefore, every term that refers to the right side of his body has the word "skating" in front of it. For example, his right foot, knee, hip, and shoulder are his "skating foot," "skating knee," "skating hip," and "skating shoulder." The side that is off the ice is known as the "free side." In this position, the left foot is the "free foot," and the left knee, hip, and shoulder all have the word "free" in front of them.

This exercise—gliding on one skate—will help to improve your balance. The majority of skaters, even those who are experienced, have a natural tendency to balance on one skate better than the other. To correct this imbalance, you must become equally comfortable gliding on both sides.

1

2

Your starting position is the same for gliding on two feet as for doing the dip—you stand erect, your feet are together, your arms are in front of your body. Bend your knees; turn your right foot to make a V, then push against your right foot and glide forward on your left—the skating foot—for as long as you can. While you are gliding on your left foot, be sure to keep your right or free foot up off the ice diagonally behind the skating foot.

Start again with both feet on the ice, push off, this time away from the left foot, and glide on the right. This skill must be developed equally on both sides of your body.

You can see from the drawing that beginners have a tendency to bend the free leg. This is not a serious error at this stage of learning, but as skaters become more advanced, they are taught to stretch the leg in a more graceful position.

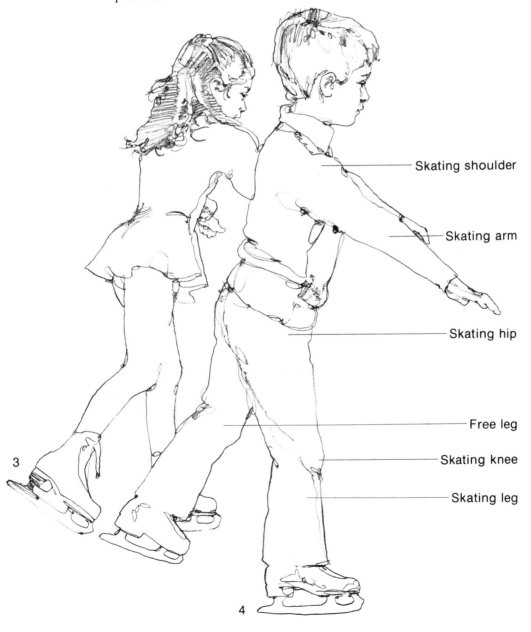

Skating shoulder

Skating arm

Skating hip

Free leg

Skating knee

Skating leg

TAKING A FALL

At this point, you may have experienced some falls. Falling is a part of skating, but you can learn how to fall and get up gracefully. Falling while skating is not nearly so bad as falling on the sidewalk. This is because you slide when you hit the ice and much of the force of the fall is absorbed in the sliding motion.

The best way to take a tumble is from a dip position, falling to one side and sliding on your backside until you stop (Position 1). To get up, put both hands solidly on the ice, and, keeping the left leg forward, bend your right knee under you so you will be supported on three points—your two hands and knee (2 and 3). Fold your left leg in toward your body with the blade on the ice (4), and when you are comfortably on your right knee and your left blade, press slowly into the ice to a standing position.

1

2

BASIC STROKING

Stroking is the fundamental skating movement. You begin with a push-off: Stand with your body weight firmly over your left foot, while your right foot, using the entire blade, pushes into the ice and backward at almost a 45° angle (1). When you push with your right leg, shift your weight forward into your bent left knee, balancing the backward action of the free leg with a forward motion of the right arm (2). Square your left arm to your body (3).

To achieve *power* in your skating, it is important that you bend your skating knee, which provides the thrust of the forward movement and is the knee over which your body weight is centered. Equally significant is the movement of the free foot; many skaters push backward only with the toe and not with the full inside edge of the blade. This is completely wrong. To execute a powerful pushoff, the skater must push with the full blade, pressing into the ice, and thrust the free leg away from the body at a 45° angle.

After your free foot is fully extended, bend it in close slightly in front of your left knee (still keeping the weight of your body on your skating leg). Then switch your weight from the left foot to the right one (5). Bending the right knee to absorb the weight shift, straighten the left leg as it presses into the ice for the next pushoff (6).

3   4   5

6   7   1   2

FORWARD CROSSOVERS

What do you do when you have to turn? If you are skating on an ice rink and are nearing the barrier, how do you maintain the same speed yet negotiate the curve gracefully? You can turn by gliding on two feet, but this will not be very effective, because at the end of the glide you probably will have lost all your speed.

Now, imagine that it is time to turn. You are skating counterclockwise around the rink and you are on both feet. Push backward with the right foot (1 and 2), then bring your right foot forward (3 and 4) and "cross" it over the left foot. This is the forward crossover circling to the left. To complete the crossover motion, when your right foot is crossed over in front, shift your weight from your left foot to the inside of your right (5); bend your right knee as the left foot angles and presses diagonally behind, under, and off the ice. Then lift your left foot parallel to your right, while bending your knees for the next thrust away from the right foot (7, 8, and 9), repeating these

successive movements until you have turned the corner. The lean into the crossovers results in tracings that form a curved path around the ice.

One mistake that almost everybody makes is this: after crossing the right foot in front, skaters have a tendency to bring their left foot immediately forward. Instead, the left foot should push backward, stroking under the right foot, extending all the way outside the circular path. As a result, there will be a constant action in which both feet are pushing (Positions 5 through 11). If you want to see good cross-foot movement, watch a speed skater perform on television; notice how he pushes with both legs, not only with the leg outside the circle, but also with the leg inside the circle.

During all these crossovers, your body has to lean naturally inside the circle to keep balance, speed, and control. It is very important that you always keep your weight over your skating hip and knee.

7 8 9 10 11

BACKWARD CROSSOVERS

You are skating backward in a counterclockwise direction and are going to curve around the end of the rink. First turn your head, shoulders, and arms until they are square to the center of the circle (1 and 2). Then begin with a backward sculling push of the left foot (1 and 2, 6 and 7). After the pushoff, the left leg crosses over to the inside of the right leg (3 and 8), bending to bear your body weight, while your right foot angles (4 and 9) and your right leg thrusts powerfully under and back.

The right leg is now free to reach toward the center of the circle (6). The right leg then "squeezes" (7 and 8) under the left and accelerates toward the outside of the circle (9). The left leg is now ready to thrust into the ice for the next crossover.

1

2

3

4

5

The rhythmic power play between the thrust of the left leg and "squeeze" of the right leg creates good crossovers. If you push only with the outside leg you will—it may be silly to say—look like an engine with two cylinders running and two not running.

While executing this maneuver, your body must lean naturally into the curve, with your head turned in the direction you are going.

It is important that you learn backward crossovers in both clockwise and counterclockwise directions. Sometimes it is difficult to practice the clockwise movement because people always skate counterclockwise in a public rink. But during training sessions, perform the crossovers in a smaller circle, around twenty-five to thirty feet in diameter, alternating directions.

FORWARD OUTSIDE EDGE

1   2   3   4   5

In the first chapter, I mentioned that a skate blade has two edges on either side of a grooved center. In figure skating, we call these two edges the inside edge and the outside edge. The inside edge is the edge on the inner side of your leg, the outside edge, the one on the outer side of your leg. Since the lean is always toward the center of the circle, the edge you are on will depend on which is your skating leg. For example, if you are skating forward in a clockwise direction, leaning toward the center of the circle to your right, when your skating foot is your right foot, you will be on an outside edge. When on the same curve the left is the skating foot, you will be on an inside edge. After you have learned the crossovers, it will seem natural for you to curve or lean on one edge.

This exercise, the forward outside edge, uses the outside edge to trace consecutive semicircles, alternating skating feet. As in Position 1 of the drawing, with your right arm leading, start by pushing off with your left foot, shifting your body weight over to your right knee and foot. During the first part of the curve, check the rotation to maintain the starting position (2 and 3). Halfway through the curve, the free side rotates and passes closely (4 and 5) until it is leading the skating side (6 and 7). At this point (8) rotation stops; the feet come together and the weight shifts slightly toward the left

foot in anticipation of the change of foot (9) and the start of the next curve (10 and 11).

In refining the shape of these curves it is important that the edge begins and ends perpendicular to the line of travel.

One common mistake: The forward outside edge is a difficult maneuver for beginners, because you have to counteract the natural tendency to thrust your left arm forward as you push back with your left foot and vice versa. In a common motion like walking, the right arm opposes the left leg. In this exercise, the right arm and the right leg move together in the same direction, so half of the body moves as a unit—same arm, same leg. This changes for the inside edges, as you will soon see.

FORWARD INSIDE EDGE

The forward inside edge is often much easier to learn than the forward outside edge. In this exercise, the movements are more natural, because when you push off from either foot, your opposite arm will be in front, much like walking.

To start, your left foot is on the curve, your shoulders square to the circle. Your right arm is forward and your left arm is to the side (1). During the shift of weight, the shoulders oppose the backward thrust of the free foot and the body tilts slightly to the inside of the circle (2 and 10). As the tracing curves, simultaneously reverse your skating shoulder and free leg positions (3 to 8). This transition must be executed smoothly; your upper body and lower body synchronize rotation, but in opposite directions. By Positions 9 and 10 your weight has slightly shifted to the left in preparation for the next curve, in which you will be gliding on your right inside edge.

7

8

9

10

11

12

13

An important thing here is that your hips should be fairly square to your line of travel. Because you are skating on an inside edge, the line of your body is slightly angled toward the center, and you may tend to "break the hip," which means that by leaning the upper part of your body too far inside the circle, you release the weight from your skating hip. Concentrate on avoiding this by keeping your shoulders square and standing up straight.

BACKWARD OUTSIDE EDGE

1 2 3 4 5 6 7

Start with both feet on the ice facing the direction of travel. Circle your weight over to your right side (1), bend your right knee, and, with a strong quick "sculling" thrust of the right leg (2 and 3), shift your weight diagonally back to the left side of your body (4).

During the first part of the curve, check or stop your rotation to maintain the starting position (3 and 4), looking over your shoulder to the inside of the curve. Halfway around the curve, the free side rotates and passes closely (5 and 6) until it is leading the skating side (7, 8, and 9). At this point (10), rotation stops; bring your feet together while shifting the weight slightly toward the right side (11) in anticipation of the change of foot (12) and the start of the next curve (13 and 14).

You can see that there is a great similarity between the forward outside edge and the backward outside edge. Except for the head, the starting position of the forward outside edge is the same as the finish position of the backward outside edge, and the starting position of the backward outside edge is the same as the finish position of the forward outside edge.

8

9

10

11

2

13

14

BACKWARD INSIDE EDGE

This is the most difficult edge to learn because the body lean must be maintained toward the center of the circle while the pushing side—which becomes the free side—is also toward the inside of the circle. To complicate this action, the rotation along the curve is toward the center of the circle.

Most beginners are confused by the backward inside edge, because while the pushoff itself is identical to the backward outside edge, the body movement following the push is the opposite. That is, the rotation turns inward and the top half of the body opposes the bottom half.

Start on both feet as you do when skating the backward outside edge;

1

2

3

4

5

6

only your back is facing the direction of travel (1). Circle your weight sharply over to your right side and twist your hips toward the center of the circle; while providing a strong quick sculling thrust with the right leg, pull your left side back in counterbalance. Your head faces the tracing you have just made, and your free side extends forward for balance (2, 3, and 4). Then turn your head back and to the inside of the circle as you swing your free side back in the same movement (6, 7, 8, and 9).

At the end of the first curve, bring your feet together (10), bend your knees, and push your left foot to produce the same shift of weight as before.

10

9

HOW TO STOP ON THE ICE

Now, let's work on stopping.

I am going to describe three ways you can stop on the ice: the snowplow, the T-stop, and the hockey stop. As you advance, you will discover there are other ways; but for a beginner, the three ways we illustrate are the easiest, beginning with the snowplow.

The Snowplow

The snowplow can be done as a ski snowplow, in which you put your weight on both feet and force your heels out, or it can be accomplished on one foot as we show here. I prefer the one-foot method because I feel it is simpler to execute.

As we illustrate, keep your weight on your right foot as you slide forward. Place your left foot in front, angled to skid across the inside edge, and shift your weight gradually to the left as you are coming to a stop. In doing so, the pressure that you apply to the ice with your skating edge increases the friction that causes you to stop.

The T-stop

The T-stop is a more intricate stop than the snowplow, and one you should master.

As you can see from the drawing, you are skating on your left foot. Bring your right foot up to the left in a T position, holding the blade parallel to the

Snowplow

T-stop
Front and side
views

40

ice but not touching it. Your weight will be primarily over your right skate. Gently place your right skate on the ice (checking your shoulder to maintain the same position), using it to skid to a stop on the outside edge. This last motion will take lots of practice to do well, because it requires that you have considerable control of your right foot to stop on the outside edge.

The Hockey Stop

After mastering the snowplow and the T-stop, it is time to tackle the hockey stop. As the name suggests, it is a favorite of hockey players and is used only when skating very fast.

You are skating forward with your head, shoulders, and arms square to your line of travel. As you approach the stop, allow your left foot to stay behind your right. Then, keeping your shoulders and arms in the same position, bend both knees, and thrust, throwing your heels to the right, as in a skier's slalom turn. Remember that you must keep your upper body and arms square to the line of travel as you shift the blades of both skates to a position that is at right angles to your line of travel.

The hockey stop is not a movement you can learn in parts. It is a very sharp, quick turn that is most effective when you are skating very fast.

A   B   C

Hockey stop

41

COMPULSORY FIGURES

Part of the beauty of figure skating is its innate diversity. It consists of two very different, yet basic parts—compulsory, or "school," figures and free skating. Each requires of the skater a certain attitude and character, and it is a unique skater who can blend the disciplines to excel in both figures and free skating.

Generally the artistic, emotional, easy-going personality does well in the free skating, while the low-key, quiet, organized individual usually does well in figures. Because of this it is difficult to find a skater adept at both figures and free skating. Such skaters are rare but they do exist—Peggy Fleming was the best at blending fine figures and expressive free skating. She was exciting and flamboyant during the free skating, yet calm and determined for the figures.

Figures became a feature of skating when our skating ancestors discovered they could "draw" designs on the ice with their skates. The sharp edges and the curve of the blade allowed the intricate figures to develop.

When international competition began in the early 1890s, figures were included. There were also competitions in which each skater was required to perform a figure of his or her own design, which was then judged for originality and difficulty. But as the number of competitors increased, the size, number, and complexity of the figures decreased. This permitted more skaters to learn the figures and allowed a standard to be followed for all international competitions conducted by the International Skating Union (ISU).

The first international competition consisted of twenty-three figures plus a special original figure by each skater. There was no free skating in those days. The number of figures in a competition was determined by the host country, until more recently the ISU standardized the number of figures. In Peggy Fleming's day—the sixties—skaters executed six compulsory figures that counted for 60 percent of their score. The other 40 percent was for free skating. Today skaters perform three figures worth 30 percent of their score, with 20 percent devoted to the short program and 50 percent to free skating.

It is important to note that the techniques I describe for both figure and free-style skating in this chapter and the next are not necessarily the best or the only ones. There is no best or right method for skating. Good results are possible from a variety of techniques. However, my methods have proven effective and fit every kind of skater because they are so adaptable.

A crucial factor in skating good figures is control of the tracing. The tracing should be rounded and skated in a consistent, uniform way. It should be without wobble, undercurve (when the tracing temporarily deviates from the curve toward the center of the circle), or a sharp decrease in speed. It is difficult to maintain speed throughout the figure. You must keep the edge of the blade that is touching the ice moving at a steady rate. If you start with reasonable speed and then maintain that speed through balance and technique, a good figure will result.

It does not follow that the faster you start the more quickly you will finish a figure. If you start too fast you will not have good control of the blade in the beginning of the figure, and this lack of control will sharply decrease the speed toward the end of the figure.

The golden rule is to start and end a figure at the same rate. But how? First, keep your body leaning into the circle. Your position must not disturb or interrupt the running of the blade on the ice. Any movement of the body that causes increased friction between the blade and the ice will adversely affect the result. You and your coach must find a technique that allows the blades to run smoothly and freely throughout the figure.

An example of decrease in speed as a result of friction is well illustrated by the way a bobsled glides along the ice. As it runs down its course, any slight contact of the side of the sled with the wall of the run drastically reduces the speed. More often than not, the bobsled that touches the wall loses the race. The same principle applies to the speed skater. As a skater races, only the legs appear to move, because any movement of the upper body is translated to the blades and reduces speed by increasing friction.

Another important thing to remember while skating figures is to keep the body in a comfortable and natural position that allows the blades to run freely over the ice. Imagine the circle as the base of a cone and that you are leaning into the circle going around the side of the cone, maintaining the same angle toward the center of the circle. If you do not keep the angle of the body constant in relation to the circle, the blade will not glide easily through the figure at an even rate.

In all figures, keep the hips steady, doing any bending with the knees. Never "break" the alignment of the body lean by bending at or "opening" the hips; if the knee is rigid or "locked," something else will be out of place, probably the hips.

Now, let's get into the figures, starting with the forward outside eight.

FORWARD OUTSIDE EIGHT

This is one of the four basic figures—the other three being the forward inside eight, the backward outside eight, and the backward inside eight. All the eights are composed of two tangent circles of the same size, approximately three times the height of the skater or 15 to 18 feet in diameter. The forward outside eight consists of two circles, one traced on a right outside edge and the other on a left outside edge. All single figures (unlike the paragraph, p. 86) are repeated three times on each foot. In the case of the forward outside eight, the tracing is done three times with the right foot and three times with the left.

In the starting position, visualize the figure on the ice; see the pattern completely in your mind, knowing what you are going to do and where you are going to do it. You must know in advance the size of the circle, almost seeing it printed on the ice. When you are sure of all these things, start the figure.

To begin, the toe of the right foot is on the long axis (an imaginary line splitting the figure in half lengthwise). The left foot is back and the two heels are touching each other in the pushoff position—the V position learned

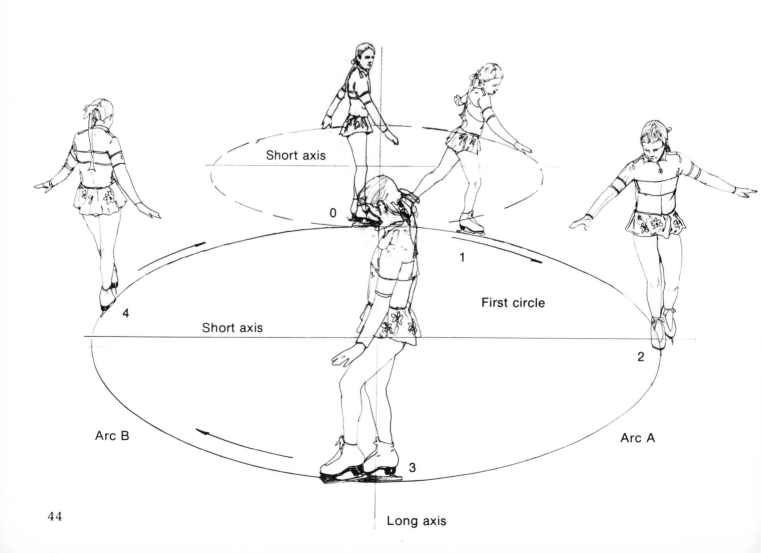

Short axis

0

1

First circle

4

Short axis

2

Arc B

Arc A

3

Long axis

RIGHT FORWARD OUTSIDE (RFO), LEFT FORWARD OUTSIDE (LFO)

in forward stroking. The hips and shoulders should be parallel to the long axis, the right arm should be parallel to the short axis (an imaginary line perpendicular to the long axis, separating the two circles at the point of intersection). When equal in size, circles aligned on the same long axis are also "lined up" at the sides. Figures are judged not only for the long axis alignment but for the "side line-up."

Stand erect, the right foot straight, facing the shorter axis as in Position 0. The pushoff (not only for the forward outside eight, but for all the figures) is a smooth movement. Bend both knees and push off with the entire blade of the left foot. There should be no forward movement of the body, the bending of the knee providing all the necessary thrust to push the body into the figure.

The right arm is in front, and the left leg—the free leg—is in a stretching position with the toe pointed out in what is called an "open toe" position, held slightly outside the tracing as in Position 1.

Throughout these positions, imagine the circle made of three equal parts. Maintain the starting position after the pushoff until you reach the end of

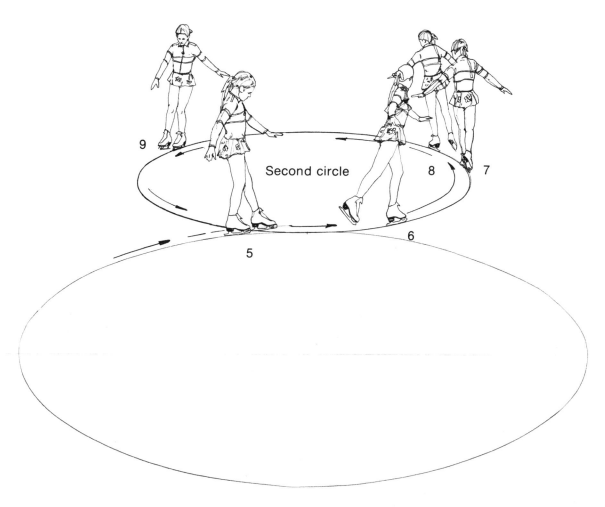

Second circle

9

8 7

6

5

the first of the three equal arcs in the circle (Point A). From Point A to Point B—the end of the second equal arc—the free side rotates smoothly around the skating side. This movement is called the changing position and occurs between Positions 2 and 4 on our drawing. From Point B to Point C (where the circle began) is called the finish position (5).

The arms always pass close to the body, not only in the forward outside eight, but in almost every figure. Passing the arms close to the body prevents them from causing any movement that could adversely affect the blades and the figure. When the arms and free leg change position, the shoulders and hips must be kept steady, almost rigid, to avoid any further disruption of the blades on the ice.

At Point C, turn the right foot almost 65 degrees, changing from an outside to an inside edge, to push off for the second circle. The body is in the same position as when you first started, Position 0, but the left arm is forward and the right arm is parallel to the short axis. At the moment of pushoff the hips are parallel to the long axis. During the left pushoff, the upper part of the body remains steady (6).

As you skate the forward outside eight three times on each foot, try to stay on top of the first tracing. Each trace over a previous figure is called superimposition.

COMMON ERRORS

The usual mistakes made on the forward outside eight are basic, and if not corrected in the beginning can affect the way other figures are performed.

- At the start, if the right foot is angled off the short axis, the ensuing tracing will cut inside the curve, throwing off the circle. The pushoff must strike across the short axis and briefly run perpendicular to the long axis.
- Another common error is the tendency to lean forward slightly at the pushoff, causing the push or thrust to come from the toe and not the blades.
- Often, a skater will anticipate the action or the rotation of the eight, which means that the arms and free leg are moved before Point A is reached. (This is a common problem with all four figure eights.) This anticipation, resulting in early rotation, affects the whole circle, causing the second half to be much smaller than the first. It is a good practice to draw the long axis on the ice so the beginner will learn to cross it correctly at a 90-degree angle.
- And lastly, the skater must always keep his or her weight over the skating hip, leaning into the circle.

FORWARD INSIDE EIGHT

As illustrated on pages 48 and 49, in the starting position for the left forward inside eight, both the hips and the right foot are parallel to the long axis. This is the same position as for the forward outside eight, except you will be skating on the inside edge of your left skate. The right arm is in front, with the left arm to the side.

When you assumed the starting position for the forward outside eight, it was easy to keep the hips parallel to the long axis. However, it is not so easy on an inside eight. The hips want to rotate—it is a natural tendency.

As in the outside eight, you bend the knee and push off, remaining in that position with the right leg stretched behind with an open toe, just inside the trace, until you reach Point A. Between Point A and Point B, pass the arms very close to the body without moving the hips or shoulders. Move the right leg forward, passing it close to the skating foot (1). Although the actions of the upper and lower body are in opposite directions, they occur simultaneously. The movements stabilize in the finish position with the right foot and left arm forward (2 and 3). Arriving at Point C, keeping the heels together, pivot the ball of the left foot almost 65 degrees and bend the knee for the pushoff; you are in the same position as when you started, but on the other foot and with the left arm in front.

During the inside eight circles, the shoulders and hips face the center of the circle. Remember that the body leans into the circle.

COMMON ERRORS

- It is very easy to "cut" or shorten the circle by not pushing off square to the long axis. When this happens, the skating hip "breaks," and the tracing cuts into the circle. It is important that the knees be bent and the weight be on the skating hip at the moment of the pushoff. If the body leans forward at the pushoff, the skating hip will break and the weight will be shifted off the skating hip.
- When the action of the eight is anticipated, the same situation occurs as in the forward outside eight. By moving the arms and free leg before reaching Point A, and not crossing the long axis at the proper angle, you are making the second half of the circle much smaller than the first.
- Similarly, you can anticipate starting the new circle too soon, cutting the end of the first too sharply. The result is that the skater, instead of rounding the circle to the center and then turning 65 degrees for the pushoff, tends to anticipate the change of foot and move too early from the circle, "lopping off" the last three feet of the curve of the circle. Remember that only the foot turns when pushing off, never the upper part of the body.

FORWARD INSIDE EIGHT

Even advanced skaters make mistakes that are due to anticipation, so it is especially important to master these eights right from the beginning. In anticipation, skaters "steer" their skating foot instead of allowing the foot to follow the natural curve of the circle. Ultimate mastery of the basic eights requires that the skater channel the direction of the blade without forcing it.

BACKWARD OUTSIDE EIGHT

The starting position for the right backward outside eight is slightly different than for the forward. The hips and shoulders begin parallel to the short axis, not to the long axis. Both feet are parallel to the long axis. Before the pushoff, assume a comfortable position with the weight on both feet. At the thrust, lift and turn the right foot so that it is square to the long axis. At the same time, the left foot will make a short thrust pushing you into the figure (1).

You will notice that the starting position is quite similar to the finish position of the forward outside eight (2), except that you are going backward instead of forward and the head is turned backward. As you skate backward on the outside edge of the right foot, the right hip and shoulders should be facing the center of the circle. Look over the skating shoulder to see where you are going.

Reaching Point A, pass the arms close to the body while moving the free leg back to a position similar to the first position of the forward outside eight (3 and 4). The shoulders are parallel to the tracing, the head is facing outside the circle and around toward the center of the figure (the junction of the two circles).

The rotation of the head from looking inside to looking outside the circle is difficult for a beginner because you lose sight of the circle as you move the head to the new position. If the position is not straight and if the weight is not over the skating hip while you are turning the head (as in 4) you can easily lose control of the tracing and find yourself skating someplace else. The shoulders are in this case not really parallel to the center of the circle to allow you to look at the junction of the two circles.

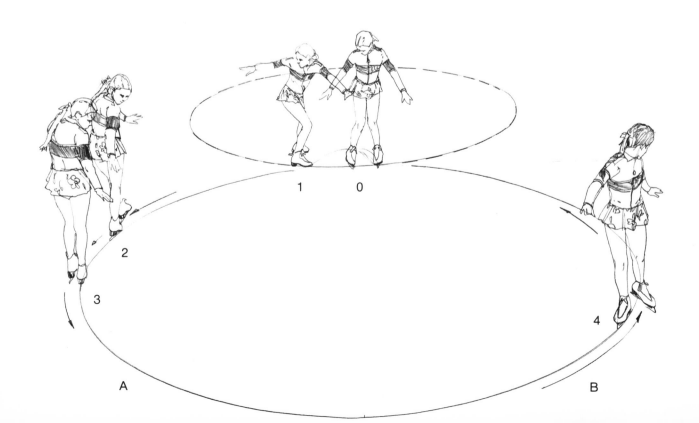

RIGHT BACK OUTSIDE (RBO), LEFT BACK OUTSIDE (LBO)

Maintain this position until you arrive at the center of the figure. Then, switch the weight from the right foot to the left (5). Thrust backward with the right foot and start the new circle skating on the left.

As in the pushoff for the forward outside eight, there should be no movement with the shoulders and the hips. The only action is the bending of the knee and the turn and thrust of the right foot pushing off at almost a 90-degree angle.

COMMON ERRORS

- On the stepdown or "strike" at the beginning of the figure, instead of placing the free foot at a 90-degree angle to the long axis, the tendency is to place only part of the blade on the short axis (usually the toe), causing the blade to trace a "hook" onto the circle. This extra movement at the beginning affects the execution of the circle because the free hip releases, and the rotation of the hips already has been completed before Point A.
- In anticipation of reaching the center of the figure, many skaters forget to cross perpendicular to the long axis (halfway around the circle), and thus "cheat" the second half of the first circle of its full curvature.
- A skater may drag the free foot at the moment of pushoff, keeping both feet on the ice for six or seven feet, with the mistaken notion that this gives better control of the tracing. This should be immediately corrected. The free foot that is not off the ice after making the thrust increases friction and delays the shift of weight to the skating hip. A short, quick thrust is all that is needed; this motion transfers the weight immediately to the skating hip. By "tracking" or following the skating foot, the free foot helps the skater to control or "check" the rotation until Point A is reached.

BACKWARD INSIDE EIGHT

For the starting position of the backward inside eight, you are on both feet, the hips and shoulders parallel to the short axis, and the right foot is on the long axis (0). With the weight over both feet, the pushoff comes in one smooth motion: shift the weight to the left foot, raising the right hip a little to allow you to turn the right foot 90 degrees before stepping onto an inside edge on the short axis.

Immediately after the pushoff, look outside the circle (1) until about one-third of the circle has been skated or to Point A on our drawing. At Point A start to bring the left foot back and switch the arm positions (2 and 3), passing the arms close to the body as you do so. The movement is completed by Point B, and you are now in an open position with the right arm in front and the left arm back (4). The left leg is to be completely stretched back, and the inner side of the free foot is rolled at an angle almost flat to the ice (4 and 7). You should always be careful to keep the weight over the skating hip. It is easy to fall inside the circle off the hip—to lose the support of the skating hip—especially on the last part of the figure.

As you arrive at the end of the circle, bring the free foot close to the skating foot and turn the skating foot 90 degrees for the thrust for the next

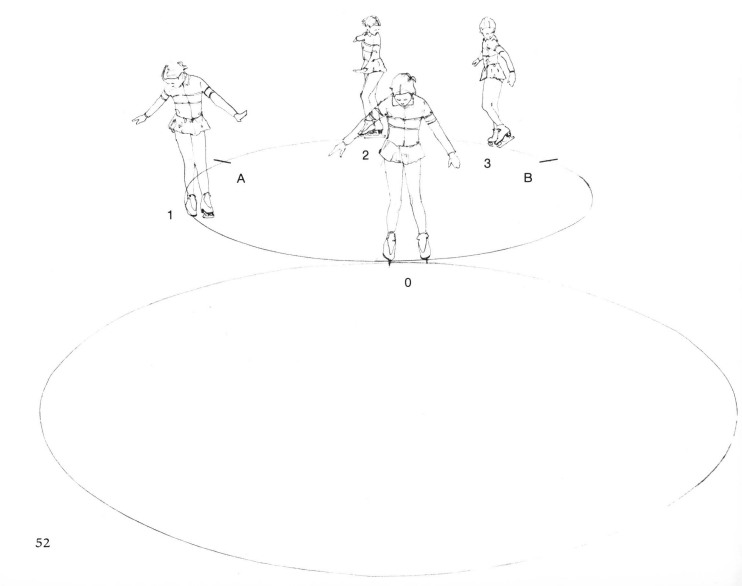

RIGHT BACK INSIDE (RBI), LEFT BACK INSIDE (LBI)

pushoff. Again, to prepare for pushing, lift the free hip (this time the left hip) and place the *left* foot onto the circle on an inside edge (5). Then immediately lift the right foot into a forward stretched position. The head is turned outside the circle until Point A, when you begin to turn the head to face inside the circle. As in all the other eights, start the motion of the arms and the free leg at Point A and complete by Point B.

COMMON ERRORS

- In the first pushoff, if the skater doesn't turn the right foot 90 degrees, a less-than-90-degree angle will cause the first part of the circle to be considerably shortened.
- During the change of the head position from outside to inside, it is very easy to drop the inside shoulder, which will cause the skater to trace inside the circle.
- Another common mistake is to change edge between the closing curve of the first circle and the 90-degree turn of the pushoff for the next. Because both the pushoff and the figure are skated on an inside edge, there should never be any change of edge while executing the pushoff.

SERPENTINE FORWARD RIGHT

The forward serpentine is a combination of the forward outside and the forward inside eights, involving a one-foot change of edge. It is composed of three circles executed in a serpentine pattern on the same axis. The starting position for the forward serpentine is exactly the same as for the forward outside eight—you begin on an outside edge. However, unlike either of the eights, you will pass the free foot forward before Point A (1) on our drawing.

As you approach the long axis, the counter position of the arms to the free foot slightly intensifies before you swing your free foot back, change circles, and rock over onto the inside edge of the skating foot (2). By Position 2, the arms and shoulders are perpendicular to the tracing. Skate the rest of the second circle just as you do for an inside eight.

After completing the second circle, you are going to return to the unfinished first circle (5). The right arm will be forward and the left arm is to the side. Before you reach Point A, bring the free foot from the back position to a stretched front position, keeping it in front until you cross the long axis (7). Immediately swing the foot back and rock onto an outside edge as you begin the third circle. Keep the right arm in front for the rest of the

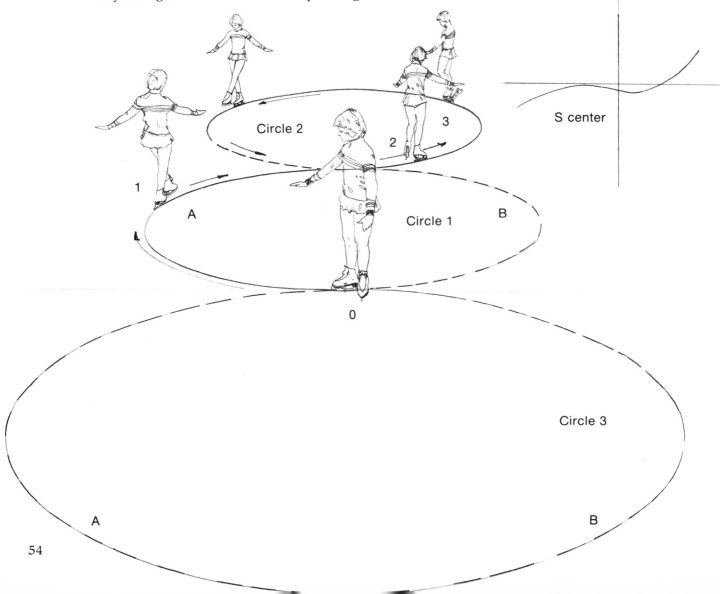

figure; this is called the *counter* or *opposite position*. As in the backward outside eight, the free leg remains back until Point A, at which point it passes very close to the body as you bring it forward.

I recommend keeping the free arm forward after the changes because the arms check the position of the hips. If the skating arm is in front, the skating hip usually moves out of position. By extending the free arm, you keep the weight distributed properly over the skating hip.

A tip on changing edges: when you change from an outside to an inside edge or vice versa, complete the action as quickly as possible, using no more than a couple of inches of ice. The passing of the free foot is also executed swiftly.

COMMON ERRORS

- Most errors of the center circle occur at the starts of the outside edges or inside edges.
- The classic serpentine error is for the skater to anticipate the change of edge, causing the change to occur not on the long axis but much earlier. This results in a bad layout of the figure. If the change is not done at the

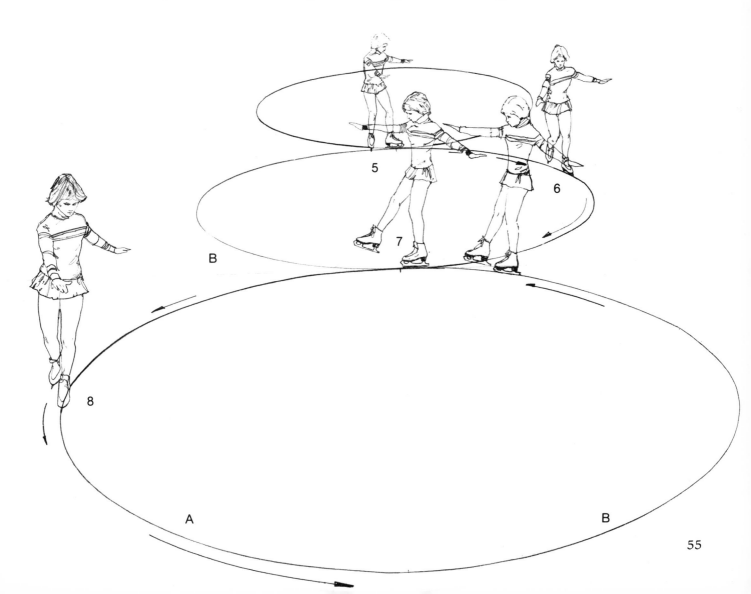

moment of intersection with the long axis, the top circle will be off axis, throwing off the placement of the other circles and the side line-up.

- Another mistake is to make an "S" on the center line, crossing to the wrong side of the short axis before skating into the new circle. This happens when the skater changes edges and does not keep the weight exactly over the hip. Instead of a smooth transition from one edge to another, an S-shaped tracing results (see drawing).
- Sometimes the skater exaggerates the motion of the free foot just before the change, disrupting the flow of the blade. Remember the free foot reacts to the skating foot; it initiates no action of its own. The free leg helps to balance the skater, but it does not dictate the movement to the skating foot. Its movement is straight and perpendicular to the long axis—never a wide swing, because that would affect the change of edge.

In all four of the eights and in the serpentine, the free foot acts like a rudder on a boat, influencing the direction. However, if the free foot is in the wrong position, it will bring the skating foot with it. Although the free foot subtly guides the direction of the tracing, a good skater allows the free leg to move as a result of the skating foot.

THREES: THE THREE-TURN

As illustrated on pages 58 and 59, the three-turn is a turn *on one foot* from one edge to the opposite edge and from forward to backward or vice versa. The term gets its name from its resemblance to the number 3. The change of edge must occur precisely at the cusp or tip of the three.

There are two kinds of three-turns: those that begin forward and end backward and those that begin backward and end forward. Because it is made on a curve, a turn started on an outside edge will finish on an inside edge and vice versa. Therefore, within the two categories of three turns there are four possibilities: a right and left forward outside (R and LFO), a right and left forward inside (R and LFI), a right and left backward outside (R and LBO), and a right and left backward inside (R and LBI).

RFO, LBI THREE

It is best to start the forward outside three in the same position as for an outside eight because it gives you plenty of time to prepare for the three-turns.

Starting as for an outside eight, remain in the proper skating position until Point A to avoid anticipating the action too early. Let the shoulder rotate against the position of the hip, arriving just before the three-turn with the left hip pressed backward and the free leg stretched (1); the shoulders, as you approach the turn, will have rotated almost 90 degrees ahead of the hips.

At the moment of the three-turn, quickly bring the left hip forward, checking this position by rotating the shoulders in the opposite direction (2). When you come out of the turn, the right skate is on a back inside edge. The left hip is almost inside the circle, checked by the left shoulder (3), which pulls back at a 90-degree angle. Hold this position (still checking the shoulder) all through the circle until the inside pushoff. The pushoff is the same as for the inside eight, except that you look outside the circle.

In skating the second circle, there is a tendency to overturn, and arrive at the three-turn overrotated. You must keep the right hip inside the circle and not let it get around too far. The shoulders should stay in an open position (6), parallel to the tracing.

When you arrive at the three-turn, turn the hips and shoulders 90 degrees and hold the right shoulder back to keep from overrotating. Extend the right foot forward to serve as a counterbalance to the left shoulder (7).

When executing both of the threes, the upper and lower body move counter to each other. For example, during the right forward three, the left leg rotates clockwise and is checked by the left shoulder pressing counterclockwise.

To execute a good three-turn, you must be on the middle part of the skating blade. On the forward three you "rock" toward or pivot on the front of the blade going into the three and "rock" back to the ball of the blade coming out of the three. On the backward three, you are on the middle-forward part of the blade going into the three; you rock back to the heel and then rock forward coming out of it. The position of the body on the blade is very important when executing the three, but if the action is incorrect, then the entire three-turn will be incorrect. Use all of the blade to rock through the three.

COMMON ERRORS

- Skaters often correctly start the figure like an outside eight, but assume the counter position too early by bringing the left arm in front. In anticipating the counter position before the turn, the body is so turned that the edge is changed before reaching the top of the three.
- Also remember that there are two actions of the three—one to go into the three and one to come out. Sometimes, the pressure of the edge before the turn is heavier or lighter than after the turn, which affects the quality of the curve. A good three-turn should have equally pressed edges on both sides.

THREES: THE THREE TURN

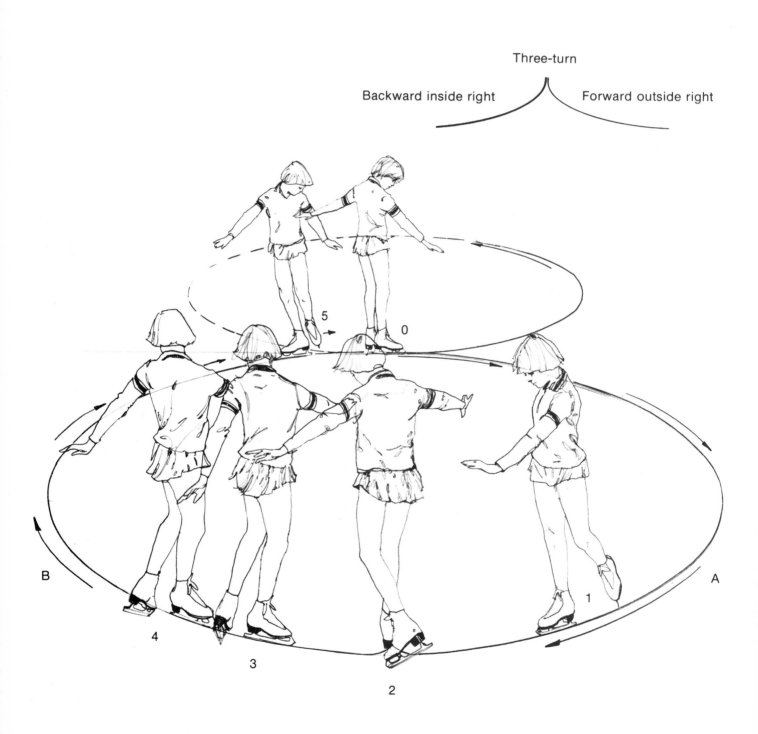

Three-turn

Backward inside right   Forward outside right

5   0

B   A

4

3

2

8

7 6

B A

LFI THREE

The layout of the forward inside three is the same as the forward outside, back inside three. You begin with an inside position as in the forward inside eight (p. 48). In the same starting position, rotate the shoulder and let the left arm come close to the body and forward just before Point A. Approach the forward inside three with the left shoulder and the left hip leading and come out of the turn with all the weight on the left hip. The right hip is turned backward, and you complete the rotation by balancing the position with the right shoulder held forward and the left shoulder checked back.

The forward inside three is probably one of the easiest turns because it almost occurs by itself. The rotation is not difficult. However, as on the first part of the three, sometimes skaters are too eager to assume the new edge, and they change edge before reaching the top of the three. Remember to check the right arm at the start and not prepare for the turn too early. Just let the body rotate at the last instant on the approach to the three.

A few words about the free leg: On the first part of the three-turn the free leg is inside, almost touching the heel of the skating foot. At the moment of the three-turn, it turns with the skating leg. After checking the three, you rotate as on a backward outside eight until positioned to glide to the center of the figure.

RBO THREE

The right backward outside three is perhaps the most difficult because you must check the hip forward, holding it firmly in place while preparing for the turn. It is very easy to short change the three and slide onto an inside edge while turning forward before completing the turn.

Begin as on a backward outside eight with the weight over the skating foot (right foot), and the left foot straight in front of the skating foot. The right shoulder is back and the left arm is in front. The shoulders then turn completely outside the circle, and the hips are turned toward the inside of the circle. The left hip is checked forward, and the shoulders are ready to turn. All parts of the body turn as you execute the three; bend the skating knee coming out of it with the left foot in front. You have to check the right shoulder back to prevent the body from continuing to rotate after the turn.

This is the most difficult three because you really have to check the free hip before the turn, and when you come out, you must check the right shoulder back. The left arm will be in front. Halfway back to the center, change the arm position, bringing the right arm forward and the left back to assume the final position as in the forward inside eight (p. 48).

FORWARD OUTSIDE DOUBLE THREES: RFO, LFO

In the double three, the first forward three-turn is placed at Point A and the second backward turn is placed at Point B. The two three-turns divide the circle into three equal arcs.

At the start, bring the left shoulder and left arm in front, with the left hip and free leg stretched backward. The execution of this three is exactly like the forward outside three. Immediately after turning the first three at Point A you will be on a back inside edge, looking inside the circle with the right arm in front and the left arm back.

Now, the free foot, instead of being stretched on the circle as after the forward outside single three, is angled and crossed behind the skating foot outside the circle. At this point, look about three or four feet inside the circle, just to get an idea of the tracing after the first three-turn. Pass the left arm close inside and rotate to look outside the circle to begin judging the placement of the second three-turn.

At this point, it is best to rotate the right arm and pass it at a distance from the body. This is a radical move: passing the arm away from the body helps to keep the right shoulder up as you approach the second three-turn. It is easy to drop the right shoulder while looking outside the circle.

About two feet before the second three-turn, swing the free foot around the skating foot in time to complete the three by finishing in front, exactly like a right back inside three. The shoulders and arms counter the rotation of the legs and hips during the turn. The edge after the turn is stabilized by the left shoulder checking backward and the right arm pressing across in front. Just before reaching the end of the figure, reverse the position of the arms, matching the finish position of a forward outside eight, by placing the left arm in front as preparation for the second circle of the figure.

COMMON ERRORS

- It is easy to rush the rotation for the second turn at Point B by moving the free foot forward too early. This early movement causes the skater to shorten the curve before the turn and place the turn too early.
- When the rotation between Point A and Point B is not timed to match exactly the shape of the curve between these two points, the turns will point in the wrong direction. (They should point toward the center of the circle.)

BRACKETS

To better understand the bracket, think of it as a turn opposite to the three. In French, the bracket is called *contre trois*, which literally means "opposite of the three." Consider that when you execute a three-turn, you rotate the shoulders clockwise (if you are doing a right forward outside three-turn), and the action of the turn occurs naturally toward the center of the circle. Although it begins and ends on the same edges as the three-turn, when you skate the bracket, you rotate the shoulders in a counterclockwise direction,

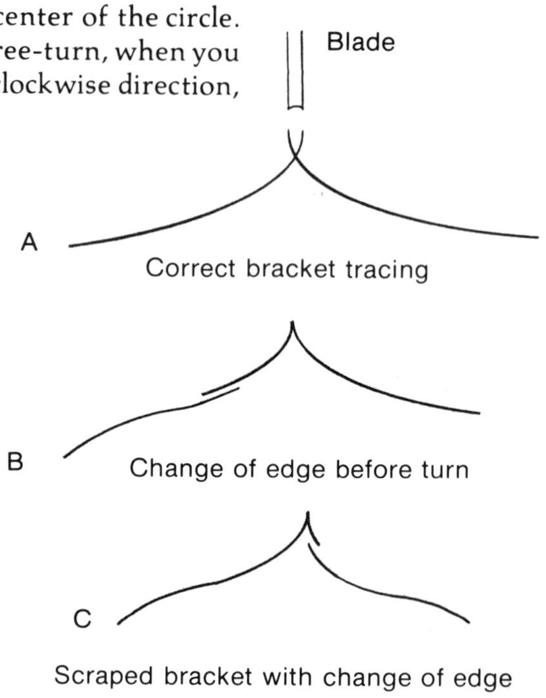

Blade

A — Correct bracket tracing

B — Change of edge before turn

C — Scraped bracket with change of edge

5

0

4

3

2

1

and the action of the turn is away from the center of the circle, as seen in A.

This rotation makes some people think that the brackets should be started in a counter position with the left arm in front. There is nothing wrong with this, but I get better results from my students when I instruct them to start the bracket in the normal position, as in Position 0 of the forward outside eight, with the right arm in front. You start with the hips parallel to the long axis, keeping the free left foot close to the skating foot.

Open the knee and hold the free hip back (1), and arrive just before the bracket with the hips and shoulders parallel to the short axis of the figure (Detail 1, p. 65). Maintain this hip and shoulder position entering and leaving the bracket. There must be no movement of the shoulders or the hips during the turn. All the movement comes from the knee and the foot. Allow only the foot to work in and out of the bracket.

It is very important to learn to do the bracket with only the action of the skating foot. Approaching the forward bracket, you should be on the middle

part of the blade, a bit off center toward the heel. In order for the blade to leave the circle to reach the top of the forward bracket, you have to rock all the way to the front of the blade to a spot just behind the toe pick. At the top of the bracket, flip the blade over to the other edge and then work your way back down to the middle of the blade when coming out of the bracket.

The backward bracket is just the reverse motion. As you approach the bracket, the shoulders and hips are parallel to the short axis at the turn. You should be on the middle-to-front part of the blade. Keeping the skating foot rolled over and pressing the edge, rock toward the heel at the top of the bracket; rock back to the middle of the blade when coming out of the backward turn.

It is a good idea to imagine yourself completely surrounded by a plastic tube, which establishes a vertical alignment of the body over the skate (Detail 2, opposite). The tube moves with you throughout the figure and insures that the action for the bracket can only be done straight up and down with the foot, as the tube prevents the shoulders and hips from moving at all, away from the center of gravity.

COMMON ERRORS

- A common error is to arrive at Position 2 with the hips not perpendicular to the long axis. This will cause an early movement of the free hip that will make the skating foot change edge before the top of the turn (View B).
- A premature movement of the free foot before the turn could force the skating foot onto a strong, deep edge, making it impossible to rock the blade to the top of the bracket. Because the skater is then unable to turn the blade quickly enough at the top of the turn, the bracket is "scraped," and the change of edge occurs after the top of the bracket (C).

BRACKETS: RFI, LBO

The forward inside bracket is very similar to the forward outside bracket. As you learn this figure, remember the basic rules of all the brackets—arrive at the turn with the hips parallel to the short axis and let the skating foot execute the bracket.

To start: Assume an inside position as you would for a right forward inside eight, then bring the left leg (the free leg) and the left hip in front of you at Point A so you arrive at the moment of the bracket with the weight over the right foot. The left leg and the left shoulder are in front, the right shoulder is back, and the hips are almost perpendicular to the long axis, as in the outside bracket.

Just an instant before skating the bracket, bring the free foot close to the skating foot and bend the knee. Execute the bracket with the right foot, coming out of it with the left foot behind you. Before and after the turn, the

1

2

C   B

hips and shoulders have remained in the same position in relation to the long axis at the bracket, so you have turned into the finish position of the backward outside eight.

The same plastic tube analogy I mentioned earlier applies here (the body remains aligned directly over the blade throughout the turn). When you leave the circle to execute the bracket, you have to lift quickly from the ball of the blade, rock toward the toe, and then rock back down the blade.

From the backward outside eight finish position, you push off, looking inside of the circle with the free foot in front. At Point B, just before reaching the turn, the free foot comes in close to the skating foot (Detail 2A, p. 65), the hips remaining perpendicular to the long axis. In this position, you turn and emerge from the bracket with your free foot back, your weight still over the skating foot. Then bring the free foot in front as you do for a forward inside eight.

COMMON ERRORS

- Failure to bring the free side forward before the front bracket makes it difficult to turn instantly into the finish position of the backward outside eight. This prevents the skater from placing the turn on the top of the circle.
- It is very easy to lose the "tube" alignment just after the backward turn by shifting the weight forward and breaking at the hips. This causes the shape of the curves entering and leaving the bracket to be distorted.

FORWARD OUTSIDE LOOP: RFO, LFO

Every circle has a rotation, and the circle with a loop has an additional rotation inside it as illustrated on pages 68 and 69. In order to maintain the rotation of the larger circle, the skater must accelerate toward the top of the loop and then decelerate when returning to the larger circle. This combination of acceleration and deceleration creates the characteristic teardrop shape.

The circle that contains a loop should approximately equal the height of the skater (very tall or very short skaters will make circles that are, respectively, slightly smaller and slightly larger than their heights). The loop itself should be one-third the size of the circle (see the detail, p. 68). The teardrop shape is divided exactly in half by the long axis.

Start the forward outside loop in a counter position: the shoulders and hips are positioned like the starting position of an outside eight. However, when you start on the right foot, the left arm is in front (0). More action of the knee is required than on a regular forward eight pushoff. Your weight must be over the skating hip and the knee must be bent. Starting on the right foot, rotate the left shoulder in a clockwise direction during the loop (2).

When you arrive at the entrance to the loop, the weight must be over the right hip. At the top of the loop (3), the free leg is fully extended and almost on the long axis. Coming out of the loop, the free leg will swing close to the right leg and then finish in a checking position (4 and 5); the arms have reversed during the swing forward of the free leg, so the right arm (instead of the left) will be in front (6). This position allows you to begin the second loop on the left foot with the right arm in front and the left arm back. The action of the skating foot in executing the loop requires some complicated movements because you must balance yourself on the front part of the blade. As you leave the circle for the loop, rock from the middle part of the blade, on which you have been skating, to that part of the blade very close to the toe. Since the loop is so small it must be skated on the front part of the blade (which is more rounded than the middle of the blade).

It is absolutely essential when doing the loop that the weight be on the skating hip. Since the circle is so small, proper placement of the weight cannot be overemphasized.

COMMON ERRORS

- An easy mistake to make is to lean outside of the circle before the loop with the weight off the skating hip. This position makes it almost impossible to do the loop.
- It is common to slide along the ice on the heel of the blade. When you reach the top of the loop, crossing the long axis, any movement of the body weight off the hip will result in a backward shift to the heel of the blade, causing you to slide off the tracing. The result is a loop with a much larger shoulder that disrupts the line of the circle. When the shoulders of the loop are not even the entire figure is crooked since the figure is not distributed evenly on its long axis. (See the diagram on this drawing.)

FORWARD OUTSIDE LOOP

Top view of loop shape and placement in circle. Note that the loop itself from cross to tip is nearly one-third of the circle length from the cross.

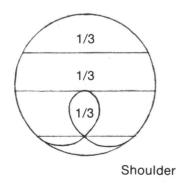

Shoulder

5

4

6

7

11

12

10

13

FORWARD INSIDE LOOP: RFI, LFI

Note: Refer to the serpentine loop, p. 76, for an illustration of many of the positions described for this figure.

The forward inside loop is started on an inside position as in the inside eight, except the arms are reversed. The right foot is on a forward inside edge; the right arm is in front, the left arm is back, and the shoulders are turned almost parallel to the short axis. The weight remains over the skating hip throughout the figure.

At the beginning, the free leg is held behind the skating foot until the entrance to the loop, when it comes forward so that the toe touches the heel and follows the action of the skating foot. The free foot tracks the action of the skating foot to the top of the loop, at which point the toes of both skates should almost touch (see Positions 2 and 3, p. 76). Having passed the top of the loop, the skating knee bends and pushes into the ice while the free foot draws forward (4) across to the outside of the tracing and the free leg extends firmly forward into the center (5).

The difference between the outside loop and the inside loop is that the free leg is outside the circle for the outside loop and inside the circle for the inside loop. The action of the skating foot is exactly the same as for an outside loop—the figure is begun in the middle of the blade. The skater rocks forward to the front of the blade on an inside edge to skate the top of the loop, and rocks back onto the middle of the blade coming out of the loop.

COMMON ERRORS

- The mistakes for the forward inside loop are the same as for the outside loop. It is very easy to fall inside the circle, causing the weight to come off the hip.
- Another common error is to move the free foot during the execution of the loop. Let the free foot follow the action of the skating foot; if it moves in anticipation of the action, it will disrupt the tracing of the loop, automatically releasing the weight from the skating hip.

BACKWARD OUTSIDE LOOP: LBO, RBO

There are two ways to begin the backward outside loop. Traditionally, it has started like a backward outside eight, with the same pushoff but, naturally, a shorter thrust because the circle is smaller. Recently, a new start has been developed that has proven effective. It is called the "Schafer pushoff."

As illustrated on pages 72 and 73, stand as in Position 0 with the feet together and the hips parallel to the short axis. Just prior to the start, raise the left foot and place it on the short axis, keeping the right foot straight (1). The strike is made by the left leg, on the short axis, by bending the skating knee as the weight transfers during the push. The weight is directly over the skating hip, and the free foot follows the action of the skating foot. The free leg, which has trailed in one position along the major curve of the circle, swings outside of the circle and leads it back into the circle (2, 3, and 4). As the free leg passes backward, reverse the position of the arms (between 3 and 4), change the lean and prepare to start the next circle with the right foot.

When you finish the first circle, the right arm is in front and the left arm is back. Place the right foot behind the left the moment that the left knee bends and the left foot turns 90 degrees, pushing off as you did for the first circle (6).

The action of the skating foot is the same as in the forward loop. The figure is begun on the middle part of the blade. Upon reaching the top of the loop, rock very far forward on the blade (3 and 8). Whenever you release the counter pulls, the rotation of the loop occurs (8) and you rock back toward the middle of the blade as you return to the circle from the loop.

This movement of the blade is less difficult to do in the backward loop than in the forward loop because counterbalance is easier to create while going backward, causing the weight to be balanced on the front of the blade. It is more difficult to maintain your balance and control going forward, using only the front part of the blade.

COMMON ERRORS

The usual mistakes of the backward outside loop are the same as those of the forward outside loop.

- You must be careful not to release the weight from the skating hip, letting the body swing over the figure. Once any amount of control is lost, it is hard to reestablish.
- It is important not to let the free leg get ahead. When the long axis is crossed, the free leg should be on the long axis too (as in Position 3). If it is ahead, you may anticipate the loop, enter it too early, and complete it too quickly, resulting in an uneven tracing at the shoulders of the loop.

BACKWARD OUTSIDE LOOP

0

1

5

6

7

2

3

4

8

9

10

BACKWARD INSIDE LOOP: RBI, LBI

The pushoff for the backward inside loop is similar to the backward inside eight pushoff, except that it is done on a smaller scale. In the starting position, the right foot comes close to the left, almost making an "L" on the ice—the left foot is parallel to the long axis, and the right foot is almost parallel to the short axis. The thrust from the left foot is provided by the bend in the knee at the beginning. The weight is on the right hip, the right arm is back, the left arm forward.

At the top of the loop, pass the left free foot very close to the skating foot, exactly as in the forward inside loop. Coming out of the loop, the free foot moves backward, slightly outside the circle; at the same time, the arms change position. Bring the right arm in front and the left arm back.

To push off for the second circle, the free foot turns 90 degrees, almost an L-shape, before becoming the skating foot. Push off with the right foot and start to execute the left backward inside loop.

COMMON ERRORS

- It is very easy to fall inside the circle, so the weight must always be over the skating hip. It will help in executing this figure if you get the feeling that you are skating outside the circle, since the weight is on the outside hip.

- Remember to brush the free foot very close to the skating foot all through the loop. And don't forget to keep the free foot moving at the top of the loop: the free foot left motionless at the top of the loop and suddenly brought back into position will cause you to lose all control and stop at the top of the loop.

- Do not push too hard with the skating foot coming out of the loop, because too much force will cause the shoulders of the loop to become uneven.

SERPENTINE FORWARD LOOP: RFOI, LFIO

The serpentine forward loop is really a combination of a small serpentine and a forward loop.

As illustrated on pages 76 and 77, start in a counter position on the forward edge as in a forward outside loop (0). The skating knee is bent for the pushoff. By the time you have passed Point A, the position of the arms should be reversed to prepare for a forward inside loop. The free leg that extends forward until you cross the long axis, is back after crossing the long axis, and then it tracks the skating foot up to the top of the loop (2 and 3). Pass the free leg close, and achieve the same position as you would coming out in a forward inside loop (4 and 5).

Start the second half of the figure on the left foot on an inside edge, left arm forward, right arm back (6). Bend the skating knee, passing the free foot very close, extending it across the tracing (7) and then toward the long axis. By the time you have reached the long axis, the free leg has begun to swing back (8). Change edge and begin the third circle as you would a regular forward outside loop (9, 10, and 11).

COMMON ERRORS

- The most frequent errors for the serpentine forward loops occur at the change. It is easy to kick the free leg through the change and make an S on the ice instead of a clean change of edge. The skater must also be careful to come out of the change of edge with the weight on the skating hip. Failing to do so will make the execution of the following loop very difficult. It is important that you delay the action of the knee to reach the center or top of the circle.

SERPENTINE FORWARD LOOP

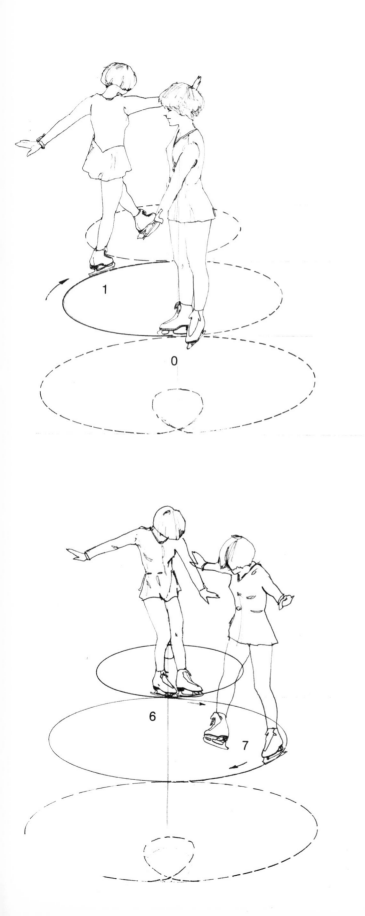

3

4

5

9

10

11

COUNTER

The counter figures are the most difficult. The counter is a turn that joins two circles, the skater having turned from forward to backward on the same edge. The entrance to the turn resembles the first half of a bracket, while the exit from the turn matches the second half of a three-turn. You begin in a clockwise rotation with your skates, but your shoulders and hips rotate counterclockwise.

The right outside counter is started in the same manner as the forward outside loop—in the counter position with the right foot forward on the short axis. The pushoff comes from the left foot, the hips and shoulders are parallel to the long axis. The left arm is in front and the right arm is slightly back.

After the pushoff, start to bring the free foot (the left) in front, but begin to rotate the arms in a counterclockwise direction, passing them close to the body (1 and 2). When you arrive at the top of the circle, just before the counter turn (2), the hips and shoulders are parallel to the short axis. This is a difficult and complex motion, much like the position entering an outside bracket.

At the top of the circle execute the counter turn (3) with your skating foot and come out of the turn with the left foot and left arm in front and the right

arm in back (4). There should be no movement with the hips and shoulders because all the action for the turn is done by the skating foot. To execute a proper counter, the whole length of the blade must be used. You must rock through the counter from the middle of the blade to the front going into the turn, and then rock back down the blade going out of the turn.

I like to check Position 4 with the left foot in front until reaching Point A. Slowly pass the foot back until you reach Point B (5), as in a backward outside eight, except in this case the head does not rotate but faces inside the circle. And always keep the arms in the counter position; it makes it easier to trace or *superimpose* the top circle, since no movement of the head is required. At the last instant—about one foot from the center of the figure—check to make sure you are touching the previous tracing (6), so that you will complete the circle before stepping onto the new one.

Just as you push off to begin the new circle, change the position of the head (7) looking inside to the new circle. With the left arm in front, start a counterclockwise movement with the left arm, shoulder, and hip, keeping the right foot in front for a few feet after the start. When making the counterclockwise rotation, remember to pass the left arm close to the body (8). Perform almost the same motion backward as you do forward. Thus you arrive at the backward turn with the hips and shoulders perpendicular to the long axis.

The free foot, which was in the back, swings forward and back in one quick motion during the counter turn (9 and 10); this forward-backward motion of the free foot in opposition to the skating foot is called the "scissor" action. Finish the turn with the left arm forward and the right arm back. This is like the starting position for an outside eight, except upon reaching Point A, you bring the right foot in front (11), and you do not change the position of the arms (12).

COMMON ERRORS

- A common error that is normal for beginners to make is one of layout. In anticipating the first turn, the top circle is skated off axis. Another easy mistake is the tendency to anticipate Position 5 and cut inside the circle. And still another mistake in layout is to go outside the circle at Position 8, thus bulging the circle before reaching Position 9.
- However, the biggest problem is failure to use the proper action of the blade in the turn. You must "rock" through the counter. While on the same edge, through the turn, the foot has to rock on the blade from the middle to the front as the blade leaves the circle, and back down to the middle of the blade when coming out of the turn. A backward counter is the reverse—the turn is rocked from the middle of the blade to the heel and back.
- This advanced figure is not easy to learn and is not usually performed well if the weight is not over the hip at the moment of the turn. Early action of the free hip, shoulder, and leg could cause the edge to change before the top of the turn, and again just afterward, resulting in a double change of edge where there should be none.

ROCKER

Like the counter, the rocker is a turn that joins two circles, the skater having turned from forward to backward on the same edge. However, the rotations before and after the turn are *opposite* from the counter: the entrance to the turn resembles the first half of a three-turn, while the exit from the turn matches the second half of the bracket.

The outside rocker begins like an outside eight. At Point A, start to rotate the hips and shoulders in a clockwise direction, and pass the hands close to the body in a clockwise rotation (1). When you arrive at the turn—the forward rocker—the hips and shoulders should be parallel to the short axis (2).

In executing the rocker, lift the blade forward and back during the turn, letting the skating foot do all the work. You exit from the rocker, without

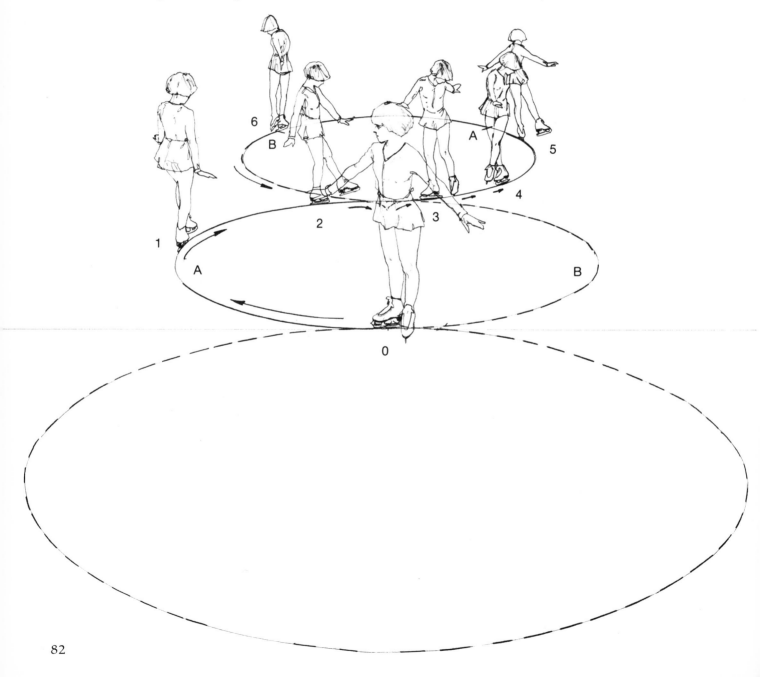

having moved the hips and shoulders, and then bring the left foot in front (3 and 4) by doing a "scissors" action (a quick directional movement in which the feet move in opposite directions and then spring back together) before assuming Position 4. The action of the foot is similar to the outside counter. The blade rocks from the middle to the toe and back to the middle for the forward rocker, while for the backward rocker the blade goes from the middle to the heel and back.

The right arm is forward and the left arm is back; the hips and shoulders remain in the same position throughout the circle and you are looking outside during this time. At Point A start to bring the free foot back; it should be in the backward position by Point B (6).

Then, push off at the end of the circle as for a normal back outside eight in

an open position (right arm in front, left arm back, as in Position 7). Look inside the circle for about six feet and then start to rotate the hips and shoulders clockwise, changing the position of the head from inside to outside the circle (8-9) with no loss of control. Always keep the weight over the skating hip.

Prior to the rocker—about six feet before—you are looking outside the circle in the direction of the rocker you will make (9). Arrive at the entrance to the rocker with the hips parallel to the short axis, the free foot backward and touching the heel of the skating foot. Execute the back outside rocker with the skating foot by scissoring the free foot with the skating foot.

Immediately after the rocker, the right foot will be back, in about the same position as in the forward serpentine after the inside-outside change. The right foot and left arm are back, and the right arm is in front. These arm positions are maintained through the rest of the circle. At Point A, the free foot starts to come forward and is completely forward by Point B. Keep this position until the end of the figure (11 and 12).

The scissors kick of the feet during the rocker can help you through the turns. (However, this action is for advanced skaters, and you must know how to perform each turn well before adding any further movements.) The scissors kick makes the turns deeper and helps in almost all turns, not only in the rocker. The scissors is performed with the action of the free foot at the moment of the turn—you kick the free leg at a right angle to the turn. If you are doing a bracket or a counter on the short axis, the free leg kicks parallel to the long axis at the moment of the turn. This movement of the free leg makes the blade go more forward or more backward; actually, it is a natural kind of motion, but it should be left to the advanced skaters who must execute deeper turns—turns that extend farther into the circle.

The most difficult part of the outside rocker to lay out is the semicircle between the backward pushoff and the back turn. The difficulty lies in the movement of the head. It is a "blind" movement because the skater loses sight of the tracing and can easily wander from the right track.

To avoid losing sight of the track some skaters use a new technique developed so the tracing of the semicircle can always be seen. Instead of changing the position of the head on the semicircle between the back pushoff and the back turn, they change the position of the head at the top of the second circle, between Points A and B. They are now looking inside the circle and always push off looking in the same direction. This makes them look outside through the semicircle. Between the forward and the back turns, they look outside the circle, which makes it much easier to trace than if the head were moved during this semicircle.

COMMON ERRORS

- The most common error of the outside rocker is arriving for the turn with the hip in the wrong position—not stopping square to the long axis. If the free hip is out of position and is moving before the turn, it prevents the turn from being properly executed, because the foot cannot lift and rock through the turn without the weight squarely over the hip at the moment of the turn.

- It is easy to make the turns different sizes because of the scissoring action of the free foot. The depth of the turn is the distance measured from where the blade would have been on the circle to the tip of the turn. The general tendency is to do the forward turn "deeper" than the backward turn.
- If the scissors of the free leg is too early, the action of the skating foot and hip will affect the tracing, making the shoulder of the turn uneven.

INSIDE ROCKER: RFI, LBI

The inside rocker is begun with the right foot in the counterclockwise rotation, as in the right forward inside eight. The left arm is in front as in an inside eight. You start by keeping the free foot just behind the heel of the skating foot. Arrive at the turn with the hips and shoulders completely open—parallel to the short axis. Execute the turn at the top of the circle. Immediately after the scissoring action of the turn, the free foot comes forward and is slightly crossed in front of the skating foot. The left arm is in front, the right arm is back and the weight must be completely balanced over the skating hip. You are looking outside, as in a backward inside eight. Move the head and change the position of the arms between Points A and B. By Point B the final position is achieved.

Reaching the center, push off as for a back inside eight on the left foot, only look outside for the whole circle before the turn. The right foot is checked in front immediately after the pushoff, while the right arm is in front and the left arm is back. On the semicircle between the two rockers, the right hip and shoulder are brought forward, facing outside the circle. The hips and shoulders are parallel to the short axis at the moment of the turn.

The free foot is forward and then brought behind the skating foot just before the turn. After skating the turn, using the scissoring action, the left shoulder, arm, and hip are forward.

It is important to understand that neither the shoulder, the hips, nor the arms move through the third circle. They stay in the same position as when they came out of the rocker. Only the free foot comes forward between Points A and B.

The inside rocker requires the same action of the foot as does the outside rocker. The blade rocks from the middle of the blade forward to the toe and back for the forward rocker. For the backward rocker, the action is the opposite—the blade rocks from the middle to the heel and back.

COMMON ERRORS

The same mistakes common to the outside rocker are found in the inside rocker.

- When the hips are not in the right position, having been incorrectly moved prior to the turn, it is easy to "hook" the turn so the shape of the curve before the turn is sharper than the curve is afterward.
- Sometimes the skater does the first rocker very well but may incorrectly execute the second or third. This happens because the skater tries to trace the first, good rocker, rather than execute the turns again in the same spot. The motion of the figure is to be duplicated, not merely superimposed over the original tracing.
- A common error occurs during the most difficult part of the inside rocker—tracing the curve immediately following the forward turn. Changing the position of the head from outside to inside the circle is always a difficult move. In this case, it is compounded if the skater emerges from the forward turn not in perfect control. These two factors can cause the tracing to be lost.

PARAGRAPH

The paragraph figures are simple in theory but not so simple in practice. For example, the paragraph eight is two circles skated on the same foot after only one pushoff. You start on the right forward outside edge, and skate one circle like a forward outside right. When you arrive at the center, change edge, but not the skating foot, and execute the second circle on an inside edge. Push the second time on the first circle onto an inside edge, and then skate the second circle on an outside edge, again pushing only at the beginning of the first circle. You can now vary this basic paragraph eight by adding single threes, double threes, brackets, or by starting any of these combinations backward.

You start on a forward outside edge for the paragraph three. Do the forward three on an outside edge and come back to the center on a back inside, then make a back change of edge to a back outside, do the three, and come forward to the center on a forward inside edge. Start on a forward inside with the left foot and execute the three, so you are on a back outside. At the center change to a back inside edge. You do the three ending on a forward outside and then start again. Because you have skated different edges on each foot, the paragraphs are done six times—three times beginning on a right outside edge and three times on a left inside edge.

The most important rule of the paragraphs is to maintain speed through good position and smooth running of the blades. Start at a reasonable speed—never too fast—and try to maintain the same speed through the circle. If you start too fast the first part of the figure will be out of control. A steady rate is required to maintain control all through the paragraph. Beginners must be especially careful not to start too fast.

It is more important than ever on the paragraph bracket, paragraph three, and paragraph double three to maintain speed. The hips and shoulders must remain motionless and the weight must be over the hip of the skating foot so as not to disturb the running of the blade.

PARAGRAPH LOOP (Forward and Back)

The paragraph loop is related to the serpentine loop but more difficult. These special figures require the skater to come out of the loops with enough action of the knee to reach the center to complete a change of edge, and then be able to complete the following loop on the other side. The common error is to break out of the first loop too early, anticipating the action of the change of edge. The skater must learn to be patient with the loop, delaying the action of finishing the loop to be able to reach the center of the change. Leaving the loop too early prevents the skater from reaching the center of the figure; by cutting short of the center, the second circle of the loop is thrown off axis. This not only disturbs the layout of the figure but also puts the skater in a bad position, often causing the second loop to be missed completely.

It is crucial that the skaters learn to wait until the last possible instant before pulling out of the loop with the action of the knee. The timing of the knee action cannot be overemphasized.

BASIC THEORY FOR ALL FIGURES

1. Always keep the weight of the body directly on the skating hip and over the skating foot.
2. Keep the hips motionless, as this will result in no movement that can interrupt and disturb the running of the blade. The hip is one of the heaviest parts of the body, and every movement of the hip causes another action of the body someplace else—most likely the foot. It is similar to an artist whose shoulder is bumped while delicately holding a brush to a painting.
3. Always lean into the center of the circle—remember the cone. Proper lean aids the smooth running of the blade by reducing friction. If you suddenly release the free hip, the body will lose its lean, forcing the edge of the blade into the ice and creating friction.
4. Keep the weight balanced on the center of the blade, except of course through the turns. If you stand on the center of the blades they will run

through the ice much faster and more cleanly than if the weight is forward or back. Imagine a boat slicing its way through the water. If the keel is too far into the water it will increase its friction and slow down.

5. Remember the image of the plastic tube—the body should move up and down through the figures, letting the knee and foot do all the work. Never bend forward or lean back, since this unnecessary movement is always translated to the blades and results in a loss of speed. Execute all the figures and their movements in the tube to prevent loss of speed and damage to the tracing.

6. The knee can never be bent too much. The knee is made for bending, and when you bend the knee the hip is kept steady. Remember that every time you "lock" the knee the body will compensate and lean or "break" the alignment somewhere else—usually at the hip.

7. Always keep a good position with the free leg. The free leg should be extended and stretched, with the toe pointed. The free leg is like the rudder of a boat, pointing and directing you where you want to go. The free leg not only adds to your style but helps maintain a steady trace.

8. The figures are three repetitions of the same movement. After the first figure is laid down two more are applied on top. They are not simply superimposed but reskated with the same amount of skill, if not more. Never try to steer your second or third tracing. Learn to do the figures three times—all the same way.

There are many methods for the execution of figures, and each can be adapted by good coaches for their students. The good coach uses theory as a guideline and builds the pupils' techniques around the basic principles.

LAYOUT

The layout is the application of the figure onto the ice—its position and its pattern. If you make a minor mistake of a few inches lining up the figure it is best not to try to correct it. Some judges may disagree, but a tiny error of layout will never hurt much. It will look much neater to leave a layout a bit off rather than trying to correct it. However, if the error of layout is greater than five inches it must be corrected on the second and superimposed on the third tracings. Naturally it is best to put the figure down correctly the first time and never worry about fixing an error.

During figure sessions the majority of skaters practice their figures on a "patch" of ice. Most use a scribe (like a compass) to put circles on the patch and use the circle as a guide to practice their figures. They then move over and repeat the figure, comparing their circles to those of the scribe. This is a good way to learn the figure, but it is not good to practice figures for competition in this manner. Using the scribe you become conditioned to the figure by the first circle you put down, and you may find it difficult to lay out the circle without it. One good method is to start doing the figure with the scribe. Then move a bit away and do the figure two or three times. Then move farther away—maybe six feet—and do it again on clean ice away from the scribe. After you complete the figure use the scribe to check your tracing and note your mistakes. The scribe is best used to check the quality of your figures, not to give you a pattern to imitate.

If you can rent one-half or even one-quarter of your ice rink you should consider doing so. With that much ice at your disposal you can place your figures all over the ice, as you would in an actual competition. This is how you really learn to do the figures. It is very important that you learn the correct layout, simulating the competition environment as a great learning aid. According to the rules, of course, you cannot touch the hockey lines on the ice for your figures, but you can go close to them. Some skaters feel comfortable near the lines, but others prefer not to be anywhere near them.

However, the skater really is better off if he or she stays away from the hockey lines and lays down the figures on completely clean ice. In competition after competition the figures placed on clean ice stand out from the others and usually receive higher marks.

Another good idea for competitive skaters is to choose their ice as early as possible—while the previous skater is being judged. Never wait until the last minute when you are going out to do the figure to look for your ice. You should always know beforehand where you are going to skate and get there without hesitation. And, once your ice has been selected, do not change your mind. Stick with your choice, since most "second guesses" are not as good as first choices. Go with confidence to your spot; look to see if there is any bad ice nearby; check that no judge or cones are in your way; indicate your choice for the long axis; and skate your figure.

As you prepare to execute your figure under the judges' eyes, be sure not to take too much time, but also be sure not to rush your figure. Think about what you are to do with the assurance that you are prepared to perform a good figure.

MY THEORY OF TURNS

The skating techniques I have described for the figures, specifically the turns, are different from those some coaches and instructors in the United States currently teach their students.

Most skaters are taught that turns are completed by a counter movement of the shoulders against the action of the hip. However, after long, careful observation and experimentation, I have come to the conclusion that it is necessary to minimize the action of the hips and shoulders at the entrance and throughout the turn. My theory is that the hips and shoulders are the heaviest parts of the body and therefore the easiest to move incorrectly.

I instruct my students to keep the hips and shoulders motionless until the completion of the turn, executing the turn by the action of the knee and the foot. The hips and shoulders play no part at all, and because they do not move, they cannot disturb the running of the blade through the turn.

With this method, it is essential that the skater learn how to use the knee and foot technique. To perfect this action, I usually instruct my students to practice the bracket turn with no motion of the hip by having them hold onto the barrier, moving only the foot in and out of the turn. I also recommend that they skate a series of forward and backward brackets without moving the hips and shoulders.

The only turn that does not conform to this theory is the three-turn. There is a necessary action of the shoulder and hip for the three. While it is possible to execute the forward inside three with just the foot movement, it is very difficult to do so for the forward outside three.

FREE SKATING

Free skating (or freestyle, as it is sometimes called) is very difficult to describe, because it is so complex and such an individualistic part of figure skating.

Free skating is divided into two major disciplines: (1) the free-skating moves themselves, and (2) how to execute them. The first is easy to teach because the moves follow certain laws of physics and are techniques that can be mastered by the student. The second part is hard to explain because the "how" of free skating is always dictated by the personality, inspiration, and attitudes of the skater.

The skating of Peggy Fleming or of John Curry cannot be adequately described on a piece of paper. The pair skating of the Protopopovs must be seen to be appreciated. Yet these great skaters complete the same double Axels, the same spins and spirals as every other skater; it is their *style*, their interpretation and artistry, that makes them champions.

Because of these factors, free skating is where the emphasis lies in contemporary skating, and in the last few years it has become more significant than figures in competition. Counting free skating as 70 percent of the total mark in competition might be a more accurate reflection of its importance.

It is my opinion that the figures are always overjudged and that not enough value is placed on the artistic expression of the free skater. Free skating is what makes skating an art as opposed to merely a technical sport. Yet judges all over the world seem to resent the truly creative and artistic skater and have not always been fair in their marks.

Free skating is what today's competitive figure skating is all about. Through television and film, the viewing audience associates free skating with figure skating, because they rarely see or care about the figures. This is not to deny the importance of figures—figures are crucial to the basics of skating. The skater cannot achieve the technical ability necessary for free skating without a solid background in the figures. By mastering the figures the skater learns how to glide and curve and develop steadiness on an inside and outside edge, forward and backward, and achieve control of the blades. Figures are to free skating what bar exercises are to ballet and scales are to piano playing.

In this chapter, I have broken down free skating into two distinct sections: first, the technical aspects of the movements, which are subject to strict physical limitations of science and the body; and second, the choreography of free skating, which is perhaps indescribable—but I have chosen to make the attempt here.

The technical aspect of free skating is further divided into three parts: (1) spins, (2) jumps, and (3) footwork.

SPINS

Spins, as the word implies, are done by rotating the body in the same place on the ice, beginning on two feet and progressing to the more difficult one-foot spins. By rotating in one spot on either one or both feet, using the centrifugal force of your body, you can spin like a top, on the flat part of your blade.

People always ask if skaters get dizzy during a spin. The beginner may get dizzy as he or she learns to spin, but this condition vanishes through practice, technique, and concentration. You will eventually spin naturally and beautifully with never a trace of dizziness. It is a good idea when coming out of a spin to focus your eyes on something in front of you—a mark on the barrier or a person in the stands (see Positions 12 and 13 in the scratch spin illustrated on p. 98). Look at that point and concentrate on it as you come out of the spin. Never let your eyes wander as you exit from a spin. As you whirl around everything is a blur, but as soon as you can focus your eyes on a mark there will be no dizziness.

For artistic flair, many skaters recently have begun to "spot" their heads during a spin. Spotting the head means that the head stays stationary as long as possible while the body rotates. The head then whips around, only to remain stationary again. I strongly advise against inexperienced skaters attempting this. It is important to first master the technique of the head and body rotating together. The shoulders and hips have to remain on the same vertical axis to keep the spin centered, and the head must be kept part of the rotation.

Spotting is a movement borrowed from ballet, in which the spins are not nearly as fast as skating spins. Dancers "spot" to face the audience, which is usually on one side of the stage, in contrast to the skater, who usually skates for spectators on all sides of the rink.

One point to observe is that you should always spin in the same direction as you jump. Too many skaters try to spin counterclockwise and jump clockwise or vice versa. (Fortunately this is very hard to do!) The majority of skaters are what is called "right-handed" skaters. This means they jump from left to right. They take off on either foot but land on the right foot after spinning counterclockwise in the air. "Left-handed" skaters jump from right to left and spin clockwise. Since almost 90 percent of all skaters are "right-handed," the majority of the following explanations and descriptions are given for the "right-handed" skater. "Left-handed" skaters simply reverse the positions.

Two-Foot Spin

This is a beginner's spin. It should always be started with a thrust from the right foot and rotated counterclockwise. While it is ideal to start with the right foot, most beginners start with both feet on the ice.

Bend both knees. Rotate by pushing the right foot forward, followed by the left foot backward, and then push until the body is erect, straightening the knees. Swing the arms to catch up with the push of the legs. Then, to accelerate the spin, bring the arms from an open position in close to the body.

This is a flat spin, using the flat of the blade, and while it is not difficult to begin the spin, you must learn to bend and straighten the knee, rising upward as in a tube to an erect body position. Keep the arms in front of the body until you start to rotate; then bring them in close to you. As the centrifugal forces increase, stand firm vertically against the acceleration of the spin.

As you learn to spin, you will learn to control this rotation. When you master the two-foot spin, which almost all skaters can do after a few lessons, you can start the other spins with great confidence.

Back Spin

The next spin to learn is the back spin, because it is the most basic and therefore the most important spin in skating.

As illustrated on pages 94 and 95, start the back spin as you would a forward inside eight. Maintain a deep right inside edge (much deeper than the inside edge of the inside eight), with the left arm in front and the left foot, the free foot, stretched backward (1 and 2).

At that moment turn a forward inside three; quickly swing the upper body around to catch up with the free leg (4); turning to the back outside edge, twist the skating leg under the free leg (5). By Position 5, the lower body has caught up to the upper body and you begin to achieve the spinning position—the free foot is crossed in front of the skating knee and the arms are out to the sides.

BACK SPIN

2

1

3

4

9

10

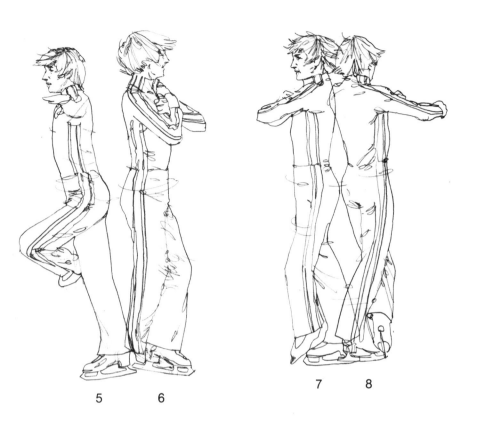

5   6   7   8

11   12

Position 6 is the classic spin motion. The free leg has descended from its crossed position over the right knee and is stretched close to the right leg, the body stands straight against the rotation, the head is up, and the arms are in a closed position. Always bring the arms in close to the body in one motion, to increase the speed of rotation.

The sixth position, as you will see, is the basic position for all the jumps in the air. So it is essential that this position be learned correctly. It must feel natural to spiral the free leg around the skating leg to give you a good, fast rotation.

Start to open the arms (8) and lift the free leg (9) in preparation for the exit from the spin. This is the same action as when exiting from a jump. This movement of the free knee and opening of the arms slows and breaks the rotation of the spin. This is very important in landing from jumps, too, because the action of the free leg will stop the quick rotation involved in double and triple jumps and allow a smooth transition onto the ice.

By Position 10 the spin is over. Note the action of the skating leg, indicated by Positions 11 and 12, which provides the push for coming out of the spin (and the landing for all jumps).

Once you have learned the back spin, all other spins—and jumps, too— will seem easier to learn by comparison. If you don't master this fundamental, the other freestyle elements I go on to describe will be difficult to learn. Use the back spin as a practice and warm-up exercise. It will get you into condition and prepare you for the more elaborate spinning and jumping lessons to follow. One of the many virtues of the back spin is that it teaches you how to break out of a spin and jump. Too many jumps are lost because the landing position is out of control.

Once you feel you have mastered the elements of the back spin, you can increase the speed of the spin's rotation. One way to do this is to enter the spin with a slight forward lean of the upper body and a bent skating knee. As you begin to rotate, straighten the body. However, if you don't straighten up properly, the lean will influence the spin, throwing you off axis and causing you to "travel" or wander away from the original starting point.

Another way to increase the rotation of the spin is to move the arms from where they are in Position 6 downward to a stretched position, with the hands together in front of and close to the body. This action will give you several more rotations. As you come out of the spin, assume Position 8.

Before going on to the next spin, I want to emphasize certain things. One is that it is very important to keep the body erect when leaving Position 9. All you have to do in that movement is to bend the knee and ankle coming out of the spin, so concentrate on keeping the body straight.

Another aspect that is vital to the success of the spin is the knee action. You can see that the knee is quite bent in Position 11. The knee acts as a shock absorber throughout the spin and prevents the body from swinging wildly around coming out of the rotation.

And finally I want to stress that the back spin is rotated on the flat part of the blade. You must concentrate on using the flat part because it is very easy to inch up toward the toe of the blade without noticing that you are doing so. It is easier to spin on the toe, but a better spin results from using the flat of the blade. All the great skaters use the flat part of their blades to spin.

COMMON ERRORS

- The basic mistake of the back spin is really the basic mistake for all the spins. The head, shoulders, and hips must all rotate as a unit on the same axis. If the upper part of the body is leaning forward, the entire spin will be off center. You must remember to keep the body line straight and not to break at the hips.

Fast or Scratch Spin

The fast spin, or scratch spin as it is often called, is a very quick spin that can be quite dramatic. This drawing (pages 98 and 99) is of a "left-handed" skater, so the majority of skaters can see what the spin is like from another view. Remember everything is reversed for the right-handed skater.

For the left-handed skater, the spin is started on a deep backward left inside edge. Let the upper part of the body rotate counterclockwise (1) for the windup. Execute a back crossover—bring the free foot around and push onto the right forward edge, swinging in a clockwise rotation (2 and 3), which causes a three-turn into the start of the spin (4). At this point feel the body spiral upward, simultaneously shifting toward the front part of the blade on the skating foot. The right knee is bent; the left, still stretched, swings around the skating leg, which is pivoting (5, 6, and 7). Visualize how the progression of movement from Position 2 to Position 7 creates a spiral pattern on the ice; the skates follow this spiral path to the center or concentrate the spin in the center or "eye" of the spiral (8, 9, 10, and 11). Think of the entry into the spin as moving up a spiral staircase: At Position 2, the skater is at the bottom and ascends the staircase at an even pace to arrive at the top step at the center of the spin or the eye of the spiral. Position 8 is both the center and top of the spiral. The more forceful the action of the free leg, the more power it transfers to the spin.

By Position 8, the free leg has crossed up and over the right knee, but notice that the arms still remain in an open position. The moment the free leg is up and close to the right knee you will start to spin very fast (9). The free leg is then brought down as you see in Positions 10 and 11. The arms are brought in close (9 and 10) and then brought down together to increase the rotation (11). You must move the arms as if you were embracing something, and then force the hands down with clenched fists.

The action of the arms must be powerful and slow—which is difficult to learn. If the action is too fast, you will lose power in the spin. Just remember

FAST OR SCRATCH SPIN

6   7   8   9

14

16   15

that you are building tension in the muscles of the arms, and the action must be slow and deliberate to do so.

In Position 12 you come out of the spin, changing the skating foot. Push out as if you were starting a backward outside eight (12 and 13). Actually, when you come out of the spin, you are in the same position as if you were landing from a jump. The only difference is that on this spin you have to change feet.

COMMON ERRORS

As with all the spins, the skater can come into the spin too quickly on a stiff knee. The knee, entering the spin, must be bent and supple. The body may be bent forward a bit, but then is slowly stretched straight when the spin begins.

- In order to gain more speed in the rotation, you must bring the free leg around in the direction of the spin. Note the position of the free leg in Position 7. The free leg is moving clockwise, adding to the power of the spin.
- Some skaters have trouble bringing both arms down together in front of the body. It is essential that the arms work in unison to maintain the proper balance and center during the spin. If one arm is higher or lower than the other, the spin wobbles on its axis and travels on the ice.
- The spin will also travel if there is any lean of the body. Remember that the head, shoulders, and hips must be in line with each other (11).
- When you straighten the body into the spin, it is very important that you not release the weight from over the right hip.

These two spins—the back spin and the fast spin—are the basic spins for all free skating. The next spin to learn is a variation of these spins, the sit spin.

Sit Spin

The entry into the sit spin is the same as the entry into the scratch spin (p. 98), but instead of remaining erect, you execute the spin from a sitting position, as illustrated on pages 102 and 103.

Enter the spin by swinging the free foot out and forward to give you rotating momentum while you lower yourself to a sitting position. Extend the free leg forward and keep the free foot in an open, pointed position. Stretch the arms forward with a slight bend at the elbow; rise and finish the spin in a scratch-spin position.

The sit spin has changed greatly in the last twenty years. In the 1950s, the sit spin was in a higher position than it is today. The angle of the knee above the ice was about 110 degrees, but now it is much deeper—about 80 degrees from the ice (1).

The sit spin can be altered to what is called the change sit spin. From the forward sit spin, open the arms slightly and push to the outside edge of the other foot. The change sit spin is finished like a back spin.

One thing that makes the change sit spin difficult is that you have not only to maintain but actually to regain speed on the second spin after you change skating feet. So you have to open the arms the moment you change feet and then close them after the completed change. The movement of the arms adds rotation to the spin. If there were no movement of the arms, you would lose rotation and not be able to complete the second spin.

An important rule to remember is not to come up out of the sitting position during the change. This is not easy. You have to push from the back inside edge and keep the spin centered without raising or changing the angle of the body. The change must be done quickly—from one foot to the other with no upward motion of the body.

COMMON ERRORS

- Skaters are often too slow in achieving the sitting position. Push into the spin, already angling the upper body forward in anticipation of the final sitting position; bring the arms in a little faster and put the free leg quickly in front to create a faster spin.
- Beginners often wrap the free leg around the skating leg. This is an ugly position and one that will not provide you with a good spin. Sometimes the toe of the free foot is pointed up in the air because the free leg and the knee are not turned outside enough. If you turn the free leg out, bringing the outside edge of the free foot close to the ice with the inside edge facing upward, you will have a more stylish position (2).
- Another common error is that the shoulders may be much too forward, causing the head to lean forward rather than be in the correct upright position. The recent rules of the International Skating Union require you to sit deeper than ever before, an action that causes the head to have a tendency to drop down. This is hard for the beginner to overcome and must be practiced diligently.

SIT SPIN

2

1

CAMEL SPIN

Basically, the camel spin is entered into just like the scratch spin—with a back crossover—except the body leans a little farther forward. Push immediately into the camel position, stretching the free leg, even before the spin has actually been centered. The weight of the body must be over the skating hip to avoid falling onto an inside edge once in the spin; leaning to the inside causes the circle of rotation to be too large and the skater therefore falls "out" of the spin.

Positions 1, 2, and 3 are the camel positions during the spin, and Position 4 shows how you should arch the length of the body rather than the width during the spin. The entire weight of the body rests on the skating hip. This spin must be done on the flat part of the blade. As the body rises after the execution of the spin, the weight shifts forward to the toe of the blade as in a scratch spin.

By changing feet during the spin, the camel spin can be changed to a spin called the camel-change-camel. To do this while maintaining the upper body position, bend the skating knee and push back and around to a back camel position—spinning backward—as in the landing of a flying camel (Position 11, p. 106). The weight of the body remains over the skating hip, and the spin is completed on the flat part of the blade, finishing as in a back spin (2, 3, and and 4).

During the camel spin the arms may be moved in different positions, providing variations on the spin. There is no one fixed position for the arms, as illustrated on the flying camel with the special position (pp. 108–109). The position is called a layover camel with the head turned upward. This is not an easy position and not for the beginner.

In many cases the beginner attempts variations on the camel spin before his or her camel spin is really good. The camel spin must be perfected before

1

2

any variation is tried. It is best to learn the camel with the arms straight as in Position 3, or with the arms perpendicular to the body, whichever is more comfortable initially. When these are perfect, try a variation.

A man is illustrated here doing the camel spin, but until a few years ago this spin was performed almost exclusively by women. Now men have incorporated it into their programs with much success, achieving the same graceful positions as the women.

COMMON ERRORS

- The most common error for the camel spin is to lift the free leg too soon. If the free leg lifts during the spiral pathway into the spin, it causes the skater to make a three-turn at the end of the spiral and to fall on an inside edge immediately after the spin begins, away from the "eye" of the spiral. It is very important that the skater keep the free leg down until reaching the top of the spiral, and then begin the camel spin. Timing makes a good spin.
- A camel spin may be spoiled if the free leg is not fully stretched. This lax position causes the skater's backside to stick out in an unappealing and awkward position. The free leg should never be below the head (see Position 1). It should be stretched so the body is arched as in Position 4. The head should also be turned against the direction of the spin as if you want to see the free leg. When performing the camel spin, picture in your mind a dog trying to catch its tail. You will naturally assume a better arched position and achieve a faster and tighter spin. This position also insures that the weight of the body is properly over the skating hip.

3

4

FLYING CAMEL AND FLYING SIT SPIN

The flying camel is actually a combination of spins: it is started like a forward spin and finished like a back spin—in a camel position, naturally. It is called a flying camel instead of a jumped camel because it is not started with a jump, although it may look like a jump to you now. It is the thrust into the spin that makes the skater "fly." If the skater tries to jump to start the spin, he or she will never achieve the excellent spin that results from delaying the thrust.

You start the flying camel exactly like the normal scratch spin, as in Positions 1, 2, 3, 4, and 5. Position 6 is where the thrust begins that propels you into the air. The free leg has to be swung out wide of the body (7 and 8). Spring from the toe of the skating foot into the air—Position 9. The important thing is that the body should be flat in the air with both the arms and legs fully stretched (9). You land outside the spiral you have drawn on

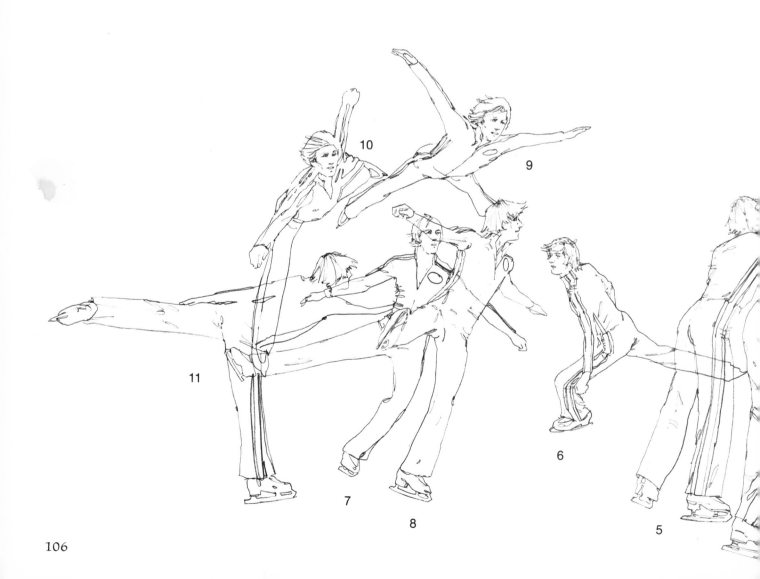

the ice. Too many skaters land inside the spiral and cannot complete their spins.

The left leg kicks up (10) just before the landing and remains high (11) after the landing. The spin is finished like a back camel spin on an outside edge. There is one full turn from Positions 8 to 11, and if you land inside the spiral you will only complete half the turn, depriving yourself of the whipping action necessary for the fast spin that follows. You land on the front part of the blade but spin off the flat, as in a back spin. Variations possible in the flying camel spin are shown on pages 108 and 109, Positions 1 to 5.

There is no illustration of a flying sit spin, but the spin is started in the same position as the flying camel until Position 6. In the air the free leg comes forward and reaches the position of the free leg in a sit spin in the air. The arms are stretched out, and just prior to the moment of landing, the skating leg should reach the ice in almost a sitting position and the free leg squeezes into the skating leg. If you land in the same position that you have in the air the skating leg cannot, as it must, act as a shock absorber. You have to approach the ice before landing by letting the skating leg go down a little to absorb the shock and start the spinning action. The same rule for the arms applies here. You have to reach with the arms open and then close the arms at the moment of landing.

It is more difficult to learn the flying sit spin than the flying camel and, as you might suspect, there are variations to the flying sit spin.

1

2

3

FLYING CAMEL—VARIATIONS

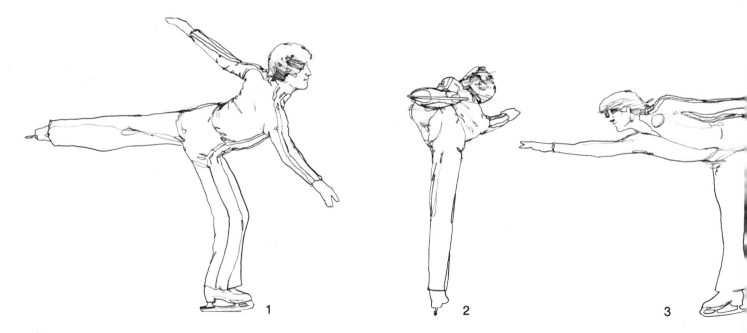

1

2

3

4

5

BUTTERFLY

The butterfly is a movement that has become popular only recently, and more skaters add it to their programs every year. Positions 1, 2, and 3 are the starting actions. You go into the butterfly almost like a back spin, but the upper body leans forward—the whole body shifts from right to left in a strong pulsing motion (2 and 3), building up momentum so that when the right leg kicks (4) the left leg scissors in reaction (5). The left, as a result, will swing higher than the right (6), and you will land in a back camel position. From this landing you go on to another butterfly, or execute a camel spin.

Look at Position 2. Note that the shoulders and left arm are kept in front until the last possible moment to build up tension, so more twisting force will accumulate. By keeping the upper body low to the ice the skater can get

into a better position in the air—a more horizontal position that is much more effective and stylish. It is important to keep the arms stretched out in the air.

Sometimes skaters keep the upper body too high off the ice and lose the whole effect of the butterfly. Positions 1, 2, and 3 are very important because they lay the groundwork for a much better position in the air. At the moment prior to the takeoff, Position 3, see that you catch the toe of the left foot in the ice as a grounding before the thrust upward and completion of the jump. If you miss the ice with your toe pick the butterfly will not come out the same.

3

2

1

LAYBACK SPIN

The starting position for the layback spin is like the fast spin position. When reaching Position 6 of the fast spin (p. 99), let the free leg drop behind the skating leg, pushing both hips forward and keeping the skating leg straight. The forward movement of the hips allows the upper part of the body to drop back more easily. Turn out the lower leg, angling the calf and foot so the inner side tilts toward the ice (1 and 2). At the beginning the skater must keep the arms stretched upward (1)—for a left-handed skater, in a vertical position on the same axis as the spinning foot.

Afterward the position of the arms may be changed and varied to fit the

3   2

mood of your program. (See Positions 2 to 3 for the right-handed skater.)

It is important that the skater's shoulders are on the same level. Too many skaters do the spin with one shoulder higher than the other. Beginners who start the layback this way will have trouble with the standard layback throughout their skating careers. The good layback spin has the shoulders and the hips parallel. The head drops slightly below the shoulders. It is also good to bend the free leg backward a bit, to make an arch from the head to the free foot as illustrated (1).

1

JUMPS

When a skater leaves the ice to leap in the air for a jump—a single, a double, or a triple jump—there are several forces at work at once. One is the horizontal force of the blade across the ice, which is directly related to the speed of the skater going into the jump. If the skater is moving slowly, the force will be smaller than if the jump is begun with a great amount of speed. Another force is vertical, exerted by the action of the skating knee, the skating ankle, the free leg, and the arms. These actions—the kick of the free leg working with the push of the ankle and the knee and the upward movement of the arms—provide vertical thrust for the jump.

The height and length of the jump is proportional to the exertion of the vertical and horizontal forces and the way they are combined. If the horizontal force (the speed) is much greater than the vertical thrust (the actions of the arms, knee, ankle, and free leg), then the jump will be very long and not very high. If, however, the vertical thrust is greater than the horizontal force, the jump will be high and not very long. This is especially important on triple jumps, where the skater needs great speed and great height to complete the sequence of jumps. The various combinations of these forces is a fascinating study, but this is not the proper forum for more detailed analyses of the physics of jumping.

It is important that the vertical thrust by the action of the free leg, the skating knee, and the arms be completed quickly and in unison. The leg, knee, and arms must "snap" together to lift the body into the air. The faster the snap, the greater the lifting force.

Another force involved in any jump is the rotation of the skater in the air. A jump requires a rotation, and this means that some vertical and horizontal force must be applied toward the rotation of the skater. The rotational force is provided initially by the action of the outside arm, which aids in the lift. When the skater is in the air and assuming the back position—the basic back spinning position (Position 6 on back spin, p. 95)—naturally both arms are close to the body to make the rotation faster. The force is started with the right arm and completed when it is joined by the left in the back spin position. The skater also stretches the body to help gain a faster rotation (Positions 1–4, back spin) with the free leg close to the skating leg.

In all jumps, the distance covered by the lower body between takeoff and landing must equal the distance covered by the upper part of the body, and they must travel at the same speed. This means the body is in a straight line from the beginning to the end of the jump. The skater takes off and lands within the same vertical axis. The shoulder, the hips, and the head remain in a parallel position to each other, as shown in the following drawings. It is easy for the beginner to let the shoulder get ahead of the body; any such movement must be corrected immediately. If the free shoulder is ahead of the skating shoulder the jump will be overrotated.

WALTZ JUMP

This is the first jump skaters usually learn. It should be emphasized that almost all the jumps are approached in the same way. It is best for the beginner to have a standard procedure to follow, rather than a whole series of approaches that must be learned in addition to the jump. After the jumps are learned well, the approaches may be changed and altered to suit any program and combination of jumps. (The waltz jump and all the following jumps are described here for the right-handed skater, since 90 percent are right-handed. The takeoff is from the left foot on a forward outside edge and the waltz jump is landed on the right foot on a backward outside edge.)

The waltz jump is started from a backward outside edge (Position 1), similar to the final landing position (7, 8, and 9) on the right foot. The skater strokes toward the outside of the circle counterclockwise stepping into the left forward outside, while stretching backward with the free leg and arms (2). All the movements are coordinated and everything must work together for a successful jump. The bending of the skating knee and ankle together (3) must be followed immediately by the thrust of the free leg and arms, as in Position 4. The body climbs upward and the arms stop at shoulder level. The free leg is bent upward. This is the highest and most difficult position to achieve for the beginner. At Position 4 the skating shoulder (left) is released, allowing the free side to rotate counterclockwise into the peak of the jump (5). From 4 to 6, the skater makes a 180-degree revolution.

At this point you bend the landing leg to approach the ice, while the free leg swings backward and you land as in Positions 6 and 7. Both arms should be square to the landing foot at moment of impact. It is not a good technique

1   2   3   4   5

to land a waltz jump, or any jump, with the arms in an open position—which in this case would be with the right arm forward, left arm backward. Instead, the arms should be stretched square to the hips. This position is important to learn because it is the vital position in multiple revolution jumps and for the combination jumps.

COMMON ERRORS

- The most frequent errors in the waltz jumps are those of timing, because this is usually the first jump of the skater's program. The skating knee, the ankle, and the arms must work as a unit. When the beginner moves the free leg ahead of the skating knee and the arms, there will be a very limited upward lift.
- Another common error is not to use the arms to their fullest. Skaters do not stretch their arms backward and snap them forward with the free leg to lift them into the air. The beginner mistakenly tries to do the jump with only the free leg. This naturally provides some lift, but it makes for a poor jump.
- The straight landing position is often missed by the beginner; the head must be in line with the body. This basic for jumping must be properly learned in the early stages or the skater will have tremendous difficulty later on with other jumps.
- The free leg swings through while the skating leg springs at the takeoff. Serious mistakes occur if the free leg circles around during the swing rather than following the arc-like path close to the body.

6   7   8   9

LOOP JUMP

The loop jump is one of the jumps in which you take off and land on the same foot, and for this reason it is quite difficult to learn. Also, in this jump you have hardly any help from the free leg, or from arm action (back-to-forward thrust) such as that used in the waltz jump.

I like to teach the student to approach this jump by doing a left forward outside three-turn. At Position 1 (halfway through the three-turn) you are on a left backward inside edge, shifting over to a right backward outside edge at Position 2, onto the circle. Now that you are on two feet (left backward inside edge, right backward outside edge), you should hold that position for a moment, standing well over the right hip with the left arm in front and the right shoulder pressing back. Just prior to the jump, the left foot leaves the ice.

1

2

3

4

Now, since you have little free leg thrust, you must remember to bend the right knee quite deep, since this is the knee that gives you the spring you need to reach the full height of the jump (4). At the time of the jump, the right-knee action pushes down and the body releases in a fast upward motion, the ball of the right foot pushing into the ice and causing the blade to rock forward toward the toe pick. The upward thrust of the body catapults you off the toe pick into the air. The right arm snaps forward across the body in an upward motion, while the free leg crosses in front of the right leg to create the upward thrust of the jump.

After you have rotated counterclockwise for three-quarters of the turn, the free leg lifts up slightly and begins to push back as the arms open in preparation for the landing position (5). The loop jump has a rotation of 360°, or one full circle.

5

6

7

8

DOUBLE LOOP

The double loop is essentially the same as the loop jump. The preparation is again the left forward outside three-turn; twist to the right to hold the position on the left backward inside edge (2). Shift the body weight to the right backward outside edge, pausing again to increase the twist, and "check" that position for a moment. It is very important here to check the arms firmly in a counterrotation in a position parallel to the skating trace.

Prior to takeoff, the right knee should bend more than for the single loop jump. At the time of the takeoff the right arm has to close in more forcefully in order to get the extra rotation.

The revolution for the jump is created by tighter rotation, drawing the free leg into a back spin position, and bringing the arms in closer to the body.

Lift the free leg slightly at about three quarters through the second turn and start to open the arms in order to get ready for the landing. This jump has a rotation of 720°, or two circles.

1   2   3   4   5   6   7

8

9

10

11

12

TRIPLE LOOP

This is the first triple I will describe, for the simple reason that all the other triple jumps take the same position in the air—namely, the *basic backward spin position* that I explained before.

To achieve a triple jump, you must naturally have more height in the air and a quicker rotation. In order to get more height, you have to delay your takeoff as much as possible by holding the backward position on two feet (Position 2) on a shallow skating arc. At the moment of takeoff the right arm has to be drawn past the skating hip more quickly than in a double loop in order to accomplish the rotation.

Basically, all the triple jumps should be approached with more skating speed than the double jumps, but the preparatory action must be slower right up to the moment of takeoff. At the last moment the action of the right arm (and in other triples the action of the free leg) must be very quick.

In the last revolution of the jump, the free leg lifts again slightly and the

1 2 3 4 5 6 7 8 9

arms start to open up (10). At the time of the landing, the free leg should push back strongly (11) in order to stop the fast rotation and accomplish a smooth landing. This jump has a rotation of 1080°, or three circles.

COMMON ERRORS

- The mistake most common in these three jumps is to release the shoulders and arms too early, and to start to rotate with the upper part of the body before the lower body leaves the ice. As I explained before, the body should rotate as a unit with the shoulders and hips in the same axis.
- Another error is to put the right foot too close behind the left foot in the takeoff position, instead of setting the right foot down on the ice more on the inside of the skating circle. If the feet are farther apart your balance is greater and your takeoff is more powerful, because you obtain force from squeezing the legs together as well as from the downward push.

10

11

12

13

14

AXEL JUMP

The Axel jump is named after its inventor, Axel Paulsen, the great innovator and founder of the International Style of skating. The Axel jump is really a combination of the waltz jump and the loop jump and is therefore one-half plus one rotation. The first third of the jump is exactly like the waltz jump; the rest is just like the single loop. The preparation for the Axel is started on a backward outside edge (Position 1). You step counterclockwise on the left forward outside with the arms backward and stretch the free leg (the right leg) backward. The thrust to go up in the air is just like the waltz jump, Positions 2 and 3.

The moment you reach the highest part of the jump (after one-half a revolution) shift the weight and turn into a back position rotating around the right leg (5). For the last revolution of the Axel, the free leg is crossed in front as in the loop jump (6–7), and the arms are close to the body. Just as in the loop jump, lift the free leg slightly and kick straight back to the landing (9, 10, and 11) on a backward outside edge. This is probably one of the most difficult jumps to learn because you leave the ice facing forward and then in the air turn backwards into the loop jump position.

The toe pick of the skating foot acts the same way as the high jumper's toe spike. The spike and toe pick must each come to a stop to translate the forward motion of the body into lift to get the skater and high jumper into

1

2

3

4

5

6

the air (4). If you can take off on a clean edge and come to a stop with the toe pick just before the lift, then you will achieve a good height on the jump. The Axel has a rotation of 540°, or one and one-half circles.

COMMON ERRORS

Unfortunately, there are many errors made by skaters learning the Axel jump. Following are two of the most basic, which cause many others:

- Most beginners want to turn their hips before reaching the height where the transition from waltz jump to loop is achieved. Anticipating the rotation, many skaters swing the free leg around rather than kicking it straight through close to the skating leg, sacrificing height. The Axel is the most exciting jump because it can be the highest jump, but the skater must learn to turn the hips at the proper time.
- Another mistake results from swinging the free leg wide: it causes the skating blade to turn and scrape the ice. This is called "cheating" because instead of starting the jump forward, the skater turns the blade at a 90-degree angle before takeoff. The upper body is then behind the free leg when the skating leg leaves the ice, preventing vertical body alignment in the air.

7

8

9

10

11

DOUBLE AXEL

The double Axel is a combination of a waltz jump and a double loop. For the double Axel the skater must get a good, clean takeoff because a very high jump is needed to complete the two and a half revolutions in the jump. You take off as in a single Axel, and you land as in a normal loop. The technique of a double Axel is not much different than that for the single Axel. The only differences, naturally, are that the skater must thrust off the ice with more force and quickness, shooting into the air higher and faster, then squeezing into a faster spin for the extra revolution; otherwise it will not be successful.

Take off as for a waltz jump, turn in the air, and complete two revolutions as in a double loop. Your free leg must follow through (4), then the hips rotate for the double loop position (5–10). The jump has to be made on a large curve. Many skaters take off from a crossed position—meaning they cross backward with the left foot onto a backward inside edge, and then step forward on the left foot, skating the inside-outside change of a back serpentine. The jump can surely be done this way, but I prefer to have my students learn the jump from the same takeoff as a single Axel. This jump has a rotation of 900°, or two and one-half circles.

1

2

3

4

5

6

7

8

COMMON ERRORS

The common errors in the double Axel are about the same as for the single Axel.

- Skaters try to cheat the first revolution by swinging the free leg instead of cleanly planting the toe pick and leaping forward and upward to get into the loop position.

- Sometimes skaters miss the double Axel because they take off and try to achieve the rotation too quickly. At the same time, if the action of the arms and the free leg (Position 4) is too slow, it will cause a decrease in height. You must almost delay the takeoff and stretch Position 3 longer than you do for a normal Axel. Hesitate or remain in Position 3 so you have time to reach back with the arms and the free leg and really push up or snap up from the ice to get more power to the lift. It is almost the same action as the golfer who starts the backswing very slowly and then whips the club around to strike the ball with tremendous force.

9 10 11 12 13 14

TRIPLE AXEL

The triple Axel is a duplicate of the double except that the skater hesitates even longer in Position 3, reaching for more lift to snap through the extra rotation. First, however, the technique for the double Axel must be perfect, because any flaw in the double Axel will be exaggerated when attempting the triple; even the slightest tilt off the spinning axis will throw the skater off balance, because the forces experienced during triple rotations are so much greater. The action of the free leg and the arms for the triple is even greater than for the double, so you can get into the air with enough time and height for three and a half revolutions.

The arms and free leg in Position 3 must be stretched behind as long as possible. That cannot be overemphasized. Fully execute movements 4 and 5 to attain full height and allow time to turn into the back position and do a triple loop in air.

This is a jump very few skaters can presently achieve, but as the technique improves more skaters will be performing it successfully in competition. This jump has a rotation of 1260°, or three and one-half circles.

1
2
3
4
5
6
7
8
9
10

11

12

13

14

15

16

SALCHOW JUMP

The Salchow jump, originated by Ulrich Salchow of Sweden, is not very different from a waltz jump. In Position 1 you are coming back on an outside edge, just as in the preparation for a waltz jump.

Execute a left forward outside three-turn to a backward inside edge, as in Positions 3 and 4. Position 5 shows that the free leg is starting to swing around with the right arm in a wide circle. The swing of the free leg must be emphasized to give the skater additional power in the vertical lift. The action of the free leg and the arms is simultaneous. When the free leg is over the tracing (7) you are ready to take off. Position 8 shows that the takeoff is the same as for the waltz jump. You stretch the body (Position 9) as in a waltz jump; Positions 10, 11, 12, and 13 are the same landing positions as for a loop jump.

The action of the free leg is crucial to the Salchow because it gives you power for the jump. The power increases more when the arms and leg are in

1 2 3 4 5 6 7 8

perfect harmony. Throughout Positions 4, 5, and 6, the weight should be supported by the left hip; the force of the takeoff is exerted vertically through the left skating side. Think of the left side as a pole with the right side free to rotate around it. The Salchow has a rotation of 360°, or one circle.

COMMON ERRORS

- This is an easy jump to learn but unfortunately one of the common errors is the position of the free leg in Positions 5, 6, and 7. Some skaters pass the free leg very close to the skating knee and often touch the knee. This is a bad mistake that prevents you from doing a good Salchow; it makes the double very difficult and the triple almost impossible.

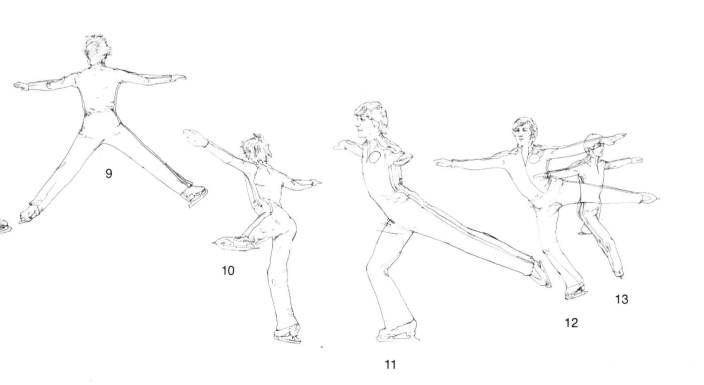

DOUBLE SALCHOW

The double Salchow requires the same technique and the same preparation as the single Salchow. Naturally there is a delay to gain more height on the takeoff and to put more power behind the free leg and the arms. The double Salchow requires more time through Positions 4, 5, and 6 to create the height and revolution. Switch to the back spin position (Positions 9 and 10). Then continue the same rotation as in a double loop, and get in the landing position in Positions 11 through 15. This jump has a rotation of 720°, or two circles.

1

2

3

4

5

6

7

8

9

10

11

12

13

14

15

16

TRIPLE SALCHOW

The technique is the same as for the double Salchow. The skater delays Positions 4, 5, and 6 even more than for the double Salchow so the free leg and the arms act in unison (7 and 8) to create the lift. There must be a longer takeoff. The free leg and the arms should turn around slowly. If you start faster you will actually lose momentum and ultimately lose height through the jump. Without the added elevation you cannot complete the rotations. It is the same concept as for the double Axel. You have to learn to hold the takeoff position and wait until the last instant to thrust up and lift off the ice. This jump has a rotation of 1080°, or three circles.

COMMON ERRORS

- Most people make errors by leaning forward between Positions 6 and 7. It is very easy to take the weight off the hip and throw off the straight position necessary for a good takeoff.

- Remember that all the jumps begin and end with the head, shoulders, and hips in line. Any slight movement will disrupt the rotation and ruin the jump. The body must be on the same axis. This is illustrated well by Positions 6, 7, and 8. It is actually quite easy for the shoulder to release the check and cause an overrotation of the upper part of the body before takeoff.
- The triple Salchow is easier to overrotate than any other jump and that is why the line of the hips, shoulders, and head is so important. Check with the left arm after the three-turn. However, the right arm does not remain in this position because it immediately follows the free side as it rotates around the skating side of the body. If you let the left arm go, you reach Position 7 with the right arm ahead, making the upper part of the body rotate too quickly. Besides giving the impression that the jump is cheated, the jump does not fully rotate three times. This is a poor technique, since it takes the shoulders and hips off the same axis.

11 12 13 14 15 16 17 18 19

SINGLE TOE WALLEY

The toe walley or toe loop has the same action *in the air* as the waltz jump/loop jump action seen previously in the Axels. The only difference is the use of the free leg "tapping" into the ice on the takeoff, before the right leg kicks through and the body climbs forward into the air.

The action of the toe loop and the toe walley is so similar that it is best to discuss them together. Only the preparation for the takeoff varies slightly. The single toe walley begins from a left forward outside three-turn (Positions 1–4), stepping onto a right backward inside edge (5), then stretching the left toe diagonally back for the beginning of the jump (6). Thrust

upward in Position 7 to lift into the peak of the jump to achieve Position 8. Land as for other jumps.

Look at Positions 1 through 5 on both drawings, and note that instead of beginning with a left forward outside three-turn for the toe walley, the skater approaches the toe loop with a right inside three-turn and is backward on an outside edge, as in Position 6 with the stretch of the free leg. The takeoff and positioning in the air are identical for the toe loop and the toe walley. These jumps have a rotation of 360°, or one circle.

9

10

11

12

SINGLE TOE LOOP

Replace the first five positions of the single toe walley (page 136) with these five positions for the single toe loop.

1

2

3

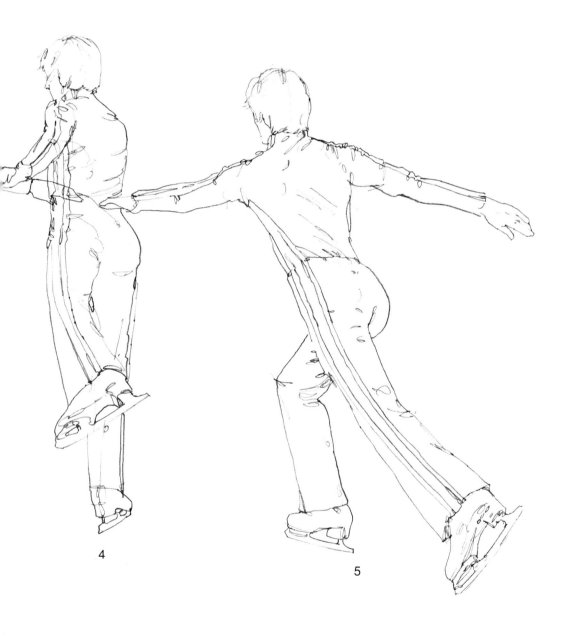

4

5

DOUBLE TOE WALLEY

From the single jumps you can see that the toe loop and toe walley resemble each other in the air. Compared to the single, the double toe walley and toe loop require more forward bend of the skating knee and backward stretch of the free leg on the takeoff. This counter extension between the two legs releases and the legs snap together, the free leg coming forward with a force that taps the toe into the ice and catapults the body into the air. At the same moment the arms scoop the body upward, helping to increase the height and therefore the rotation of the jump. One

1   2   3   4   5   6   7   8   9   10

DOUBLE TOE LOOP

important thing to remember when moving from Position 6 and jumping into the air is to kick the free leg across in front of you (7), perpendicular to the direction of travel (8). This kicking action adds elevation to the jump, besides insuring that the jump is performed along a straight line. In Position 9 the skater has already begun to turn into the standard loop rotating position with the left leg crossed in front as in all the other jumps; the finishing rotation and landing are exactly like the double loop. These jumps have a rotation of 720°, or two circles.

11 12 13

14

15

16

TRIPLE TOE WALLEY

Most skaters find the triple toe walley easier than the triple toe loop, even though a judge may not see much difference between the two jumps. Because of the change of foot during the preparation, the double toe walley and the triple toe walley are easier to perform on a straight line at the takeoff, preventing the skater from falling into the circle of the takeoff edge. These jumps have a rotation of 1080°, or three circles.

COMMON ERRORS

- The most common error for these jumps is to let the free leg swing around too far during the three-turn, causing the pick to be planted too far inside the circle. The left shoulder then drops, the weight shifts to the left too soon, and the body "breaks" out of alignment. All this can be

TRIPLE TOE LOOP

prevented by a straight line of travel during the takeoff, with the hips and shoulders staying square to the tracing until the last possible instant.

- As in the double and triple Salchows, it is important that the skater check the left arm forward until the moment of the pick action. If the left arm and shoulder start to rotate too soon, the upper part of the body will lunge ahead of the skater and overrotate the takeoff. Even though the skater does not in fact remain square to the approach until the moment of takeoff, he or she must try to stretch the left arm forward as long as possible, in order to prevent rotation before the moment of the lift and pick action.

12   13   14   15   16   17   18

FLIP JUMP

The flip jump, another straight-line jump, is approached on a left forward inside edge (1). The skater then pushes with the right toe (2), turns a left three onto a left backward inside edge (3 and 4), bends the skating knee forward, and stretches the free leg backward off the ice (4). In a single motion, the skating leg straightens, the free leg snaps forward, planting the toe into the ice (5), and the upper body rocks back until the shoulders and head align vertically with the legs and feet in the loop position (6).

The difference between the toe walley and the flip is that you tap with the left foot for the toe walley and with the right foot for the flip. Also, in the flip jump, because you take off and land around the right leg, you get little assistance from the free leg at the takeoff. The simultaneous snap of the legs together and the punch of the right arm hurl you into the air (6). You spin in the usual position through Position 7 and into Position 8. Here the free leg starts to open out on the single jump, and you execute the landing as in the illustrations. The flip jump has a rotation of 360°, or one circle.

1

2

3

4

5   6

7

8

9

10

11

12

DOUBLE FLIP

The takeoff technique for the double flip is the same as for the single flip. The snapping action of the jump has to be more forceful, and the arms come into a tighter position close to the body. The increased intensity of these actions creates the additional height and spin needed for double rotation. Positions 9 and 10 are the classic positions in the air, with the free leg wrapped and ready for the landing at Positions 12 and 13. This jump has a rotation of 720°, or two circles.

12

13

14

15

TRIPLE FLIP

The triple flip uses the same technique as the double flip jump. The timing between Positions 3, 4, and 5 is very important. The toe pick must be placed in the ice at the last possible moment—just as in the other triple jumps. The delay of the toe action gives the skater more time to reach back with the right arm and free leg, causing them to move forward with more force and adding more vertical thrust to the jump. The technique for the triple flip in the air is shown in Positions 11, 12, and 13 and is exactly the same as for the double flip, except, of course, there is one more revolution. This jump has a rotation of 1080°, or three circles.

COMMON ERRORS

- A common mistake in the flip jump is to place the toe pick too much to the inside of the curve after the preparatory three-turn. This movement causes the skater to lean inside, curving the entire jump and tilting in the air. The skater must move backward off the ice, keeping the line of travel straight both before and after the opening three-turn. Of course, as in most jumps, anticipation of rotation during the takeoff reduces the height of the jump and may result in overrotation of the landing.

13

14

15

16

17

LUTZ JUMP

The Lutz is different from the other jumps, but resembles the flip the most. The approach for the double flip, remember, is a straight line on the flat of the blade, or on a slight inside edge. The rules require that the Lutz be taken off from a backward outside edge—that means the skater comes in on a wide circle rotating in the opposite direction from the jump itself, on a left backward outside edge, as you can see in Positions 1, 2, and 3. The skater reaches back with the right leg and arm, creating a tension that releases the toe into the ice (Position 5). Position 6 shows how the skater has backed into the air; the arms have swung forcefully close to the body. Positions 7, 8, and 9 show the similarity to the movements in the flip. The landing curves in the opposite direction to the takeoff, on a right backward outside edge. The Lutz jump has a rotation of 360°, or one circle.

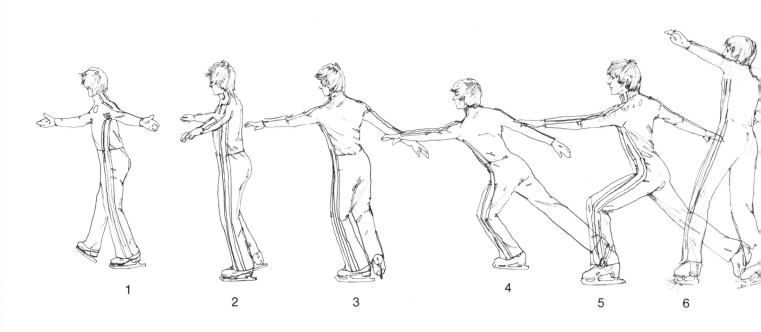

1   2   3   4   5   6

7

8

9

10

11

12

DOUBLE LUTZ

The double Lutz has the same approach as the single Lutz. Now the right arm has to snap more quickly and forcefully, pulling in closer to the body for a faster spin. In order to add the extra rotation, you should give more height to the jump. That is accomplished by a deeper skating-knee bend before the leg snaps forward and the toe plants into the ice. The position in the air is the classic backward spinning position that was first learned in the back spin. This jump has a rotation of 720°, or two circles.

1   2   3   4   5   6

7

8

9   10

11

12   13

14

15

TRIPLE LUTZ

The triple Lutz is like the triple flip. Naturally the skater requires more speed and a more powerful approach than in the double Lutz. As you reach farther back with the free leg, the skating knee will bend even more to give you the perfect timing for this, the most difficult of all the triple jumps. The delay just before the toe picks is vital for the right arm to begin its rotation. During the delay of the legs, the upper body has caught up to the lower body, and the upper and lower body now simultaneously thrust upward.

The Lutz is difficult because the rhythm is not inherent in the approach as it is in the other jumps. The other jumps—the walley, the flip, and the Salchow—have a three-turn before the takeoff. Those jumps allow you more time to prepare, and they have a clear beginning; in the Lutz, because you ride on a long backward outside edge, you do not have any action in approaching the jump. This long edge is the preparation and flows directly into the action of the jump, in which you bend the skating knee and swing the free leg back (3 and 4). This jump has a rotation of 1080°, or three circles.

1   2   3   4   5   6   7   8   9   10

COMMON ERRORS

- It is a very common error to change edge between Positions 4 and 5. If a change of edge occurs, the jump is no longer a Lutz according to the rules; it will be a flip. The Lutz must be taken from an outside edge. The pick has to be perfectly straight, and this makes the jump more difficult. With the long outside edge approach it is easy to anticipate the rotation with the shoulder and the arms, shifting the weight to the right and forcing you to go on an inside edge, destroying the Lutz. A good judge will penalize you for doing a flip instead of a Lutz. To prevent changing the edge before takeoff, remember to stretch forward with the left arm and have the feeling that you are holding onto something in front of you with the left hand. The position in the air is the classic backward spinning position and is stretched the same as the other triple jumps. You land the Lutz on a backward outside edge on the right foot. During the Lutz, from the top of the ice rink the skater appears to make a big "S" on the ice, whereas during the flip and the toe loops the skater makes a straight line.

11

12   13

14

15

16

17

BACKWARD SOMERSAULT

Acrobatic Skating

Acrobatic skating takes moves from gymnastics and adapts them to the ice. Surely they take nothing away from artistic skating, yet they add tremendous variety and personality to the program. The audience effect from a somersault jump, for example, is fantastic; after all, skating is presented not only to a panel of judges but also to a paying audience of fifteen to twenty thousand.

The backward somersault illustrated here is seen at every professional ice show, but it has been performed only once in amateur competition. It was probably banned because the International Skating Union felt the jump was not really a skating jump, as it is taken off and landed on two feet instead of one. Another reason may be that it is a dangerous jump, because the head turns over the heels.

It is hoped that in the future the skating community will reexamine these moves and allow them into competition to add excitement and variety to the sport of free skating.

FREE-SKATING PROGRAMS IN COMPETITION

In free-skating competition, a well-balanced program of free-skating components—jumps, spins, steps, and other linking movements-with a minimum of two-footed skating is performed to music of the skater's choice. The free-skating competition at the junior and senior levels is divided into two separate sections, called the short program and the long program.

The Short Program

The short program consists of seven required elements that must be executed in any order within two minutes or less.

The seven classes of elements for senior levels from which the International Skating Union selects each season are: a double jump; a double Axel; a two-jump combination, consisting of a double jump together with the same or any other double or triple jump; a flying spin; a camel, sit, or flying sit spin, with one change of foot; a spin combination with one change of foot and two changes of position; and a footwork or step sequence (skated on a straight line, serpentine, or circular pattern). Each year the element changes: the double jump one year may be a double flip and the following year a double loop. It is possible that the ISU will add triple jumps to the short program in the near future.

Two marks are awarded by a panel of judges on a scale of 0 to 6, of which 0 is "not skated" and 6 is "perfect and faultless." From each judge, the skater receives one mark for a technical merit and one for artistic impression. The judges will impose a penalty, according to the degree of difficulty of the element, if any one of the seven elements is missing or not completed. If the skater wrongly executes one of the elements, he or she cannot go back to try to repeat it correctly.

In the short program (as well as the long), the choice of music and the choreography are important. Usually, a relatively fast-tempoed musical composition is selected in order to execute the required number of elements within the allotted two minutes.

It is my opinion that choreography in the short program has improved in the last couple of years. Skaters and their coaches seem much more willing to experiment with different types of music, such as ethnic music, that is well suited to the two-minute-or-less format. One sees more original and interesting arrangements of the required seven elements. The usual advice I give my skaters is to start and finish with two of the most important, i.e., the most difficult, elements (the combination jump, for example). I do not recommend skating the jumps consecutively, because while you are executing the second, the judge may still be marking you on the first and not notice your performance. I would suggest alternating jumps with a spin or some footwork. It is important that the short program give the effect of one concise statement.

The Long Program

The long program consists of free-skating components with no required elements. The coach and skater have free rein over choreography and music for the five-minute program.

The skater is judged on technical merit and artistic expression. Jumps and spins must be included, and they must be well synchronized to the music. To give the program balance, jumps should be distributed throughout the duration of the program. If a skater can demonstrate the ability to execute a certain jump at least once, this jump should not be repeated throughout the program. The rest of the time should be devoted to choreography, musical composition, spinning, and footwork. The skater should make sure the program is well balanced. A good way to do this is to diagram the entire program, from start to finish, on a piece of paper. You can then see for yourself if all the jumps and spins are equally distributed on the ice surface.

CHOREOGRAPHY

Choice of Music

I prefer that skaters, especially advanced skaters, choose their own music at the beginning of the summer season. This is very important for several reasons. First, the skater must skate the program with genuine feeling and understanding. In order to do this the skater must respond to the music that accompanies the performance. The music must adequately express the feelings and images the skater wishes to communicate.

The musical composition of the program is usually begun with a fast tempo, shifting to a slow movement and picking up with a fast ending. Sometimes you can vary the musical format: a soft, slow beginning moving into a stronger rhythm may then shift into quick, light music for footwork, becoming slow again—only to move into a strong and vibrant ending. I usually stay away from such alternating programs. In senior competitions I like a strong, fast beginning, a slow tempo for about two minutes, a short insert of light music with an instrument like a flute (good accompaniment for footwork), and then a strong, fast ending. (Only if a skater is extremely artistic would I suggest a slow ending; you must be able to involve the audience in the drama of your movement. "Silencing" the audience with the intensity of your movement, you surprise them by ending—breaking the spell—eliciting spontaneous applause.)

The transition from one piece to another is very important. The skater should choose pieces of music that are similar in style and tone so the

EXPRESSIVE MOVES <italic>(continued)</italic>

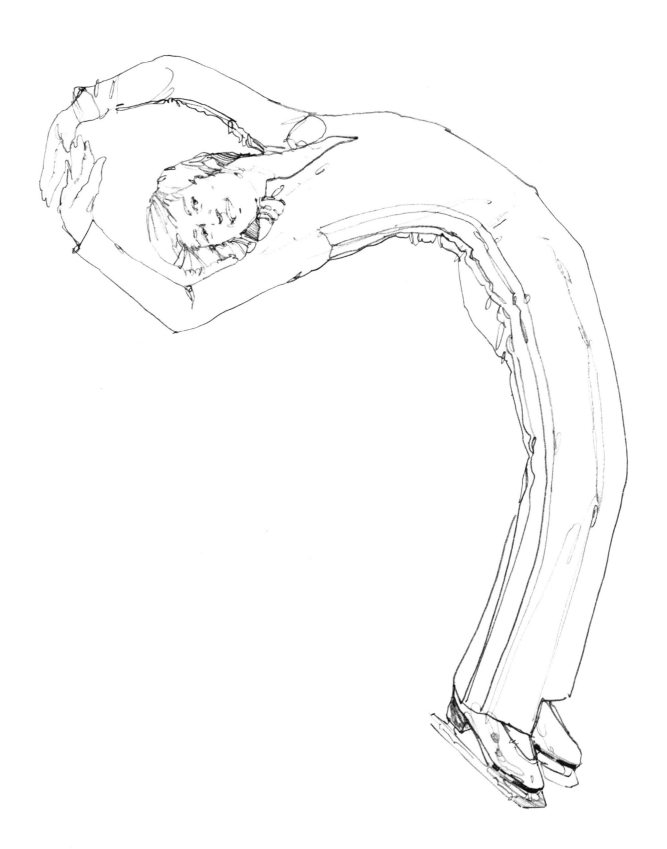

musical transitions are not jarring. I cannot understand the practice of using classical music in the opening of the program, then switching to disco, and finally returning to classical again. The audience and judges are bewildered and upset by the sudden change of style. Nor do I appreciate the device of choosing music that is extremely well known, only to alternate with obscure music that few have ever heard. When the music is disjointed, the skater's performance will appear fragmented. Therefore, it is important to be consistent when choosing musical compositions.

Furthermore, an experienced technician should splice the musical selections together and not allow harsh notes to be heard. Some skaters choose to begin a performance with a warning note or "bleep," like one who is starting a race. I think there should be a short, five-to-ten-second musical introduction that indicates when the program is to commence. It is so much more artistic than a bleep.

Expressive Qualities

Choreography is something very personal, and every individual skater should have some little trademark that separates him or her from the others. The skater must develop the ability to interpret the music with feeling. This will make the difference between a great champion and a mediocre skater. Appropriate expression of the character of the music determines the artistic level of the program. Too often you see movements whose quality has no connection to the music, no matter how well performed by the skater. The skater's ultimate goal regarding the artistic aspect of the program is to allow the music to evoke the character of the movements, showing that what the skater is doing technically is relevant to the performance as a whole. Sometimes you witness very good movements and sequences that are insignificant as far as the music is concerned. The melting of these movements from one to the other creates the choreography of the program.

Another very important element is the execution of the program. A program may be well choreographed and synchronized with the music, but when you see it performed on two different occasions, you don't realize it is the same program. The choreography might be perfect, but at one of the performances the skater lacks a special emotional feeling, a feeling that would have made the performance exceptional. The skater must communicate with the public, establish a relationship, like a great actor. The way the skater carries the head, the way he or she lands after a jump, the way the facial expressions reflect the mood, along with the music and the movement of the hands and body, all play an integral role in the audience response. If the skater can project inner attitudes and feelings, he or she will gain rapport with the audience. The lack of this communication and intensity can make a tremendous difference in the performance. Skaters must be in touch with their feelings and be willing to express them as they step onto the ice.

NUTRITION and COMPETITIVE SKATERS

by Dr. Hugh C. Graham, Jr.

Vice Chairman, Sports Medicine Committee,
The United States Figure Skating Association

The basic nutritional needs of skaters in vigorous competitive skating do not differ from the needs of any athlete in training. A training diet must provide for maintenance of an ideal and efficient body weight and meet the energy requirements of training. The caloric expenditure of each skater varies with body size, metabolic rate, and the duration and intensity of the training regimen. Usually 500 to 1,500 calories are added to normal daily caloric requirements. Adolescents and young adult males of ideal weight regularly consume 3,000 calories per day, while females consume 2,100 calories per day.

All nutritional authorities agree that there is no single best food for athletes and that an ideal, balanced diet consists of 15 percent of calories derived from protein, 50 to 55 percent from carbohydrates, and 30 to 35 percent from fat. The emphasis is on carbohydrates, since they are the basic source of muscle glycogen, the most efficient body fuel. It is also important to emphasize that protein supplements or meals heavy in protein are not needed for top athletic performance. Skaters should obtain a list of the basic food groups, so that these recommendations can be translated into daily portions of foods.

It is important to avoid gas-forming foods such as cabbage, beans, onions, and carbonated drinks, especially before vigorous exercise or competition. The precompetition meal should be three hours prior to skating, allowing for proper digestion and absorption. It should be bland, nongreasy, and high in carbohydrate, avoiding excessive fat and protein.

There is no reliable evidence linking improved performance with high doses of vitamins. There is considerable evidence of toxicity with excessive vitamin consumption, especially of fat-soluble vitamins. A well-balanced diet will supply all the recommended vitamins and minerals for athletic performance. It is most important for coaches and parents to help the skater avoid fad diets and magic supplements that promise great performance.

COMPETITIONS

Figure-skating competitions began during the second half of the nineteenth century, when figure-skating clubs first spread through Europe—the first, the Edinburgh Skating Club, was formed in Scotland in 1742. Initially, clubs conducted their own internal contests, and that naturally led to rivalry between clubs, leading eventually to national championships.

In the beginning there were several kinds of skating contests. There were special competitions in "fancy" skating, which was the drawing of complex figures on the ice. The figures were judged for their beauty, originality, symmetry of design, and difficulty of execution. Fancy skating continued into the twentieth century, although the last major international competition in fancy skating (or "special figures," as it was also called) was in the 1908 Olympic Games, where N. Kolomenkin of Russia won the gold medal for his special figures.

There were also competitions to determine who could jump over the greatest number of top hats placed carefully upon the ice. This was a forerunner of today's barrel-jumping contests. There were skating races (which developed into a legitimate sport in its own right) and "artistic skating."

Artistic skating was the root of the international style first exhibited by Jackson Haines in the 1870s. It was an interpretive kind of skating, combining the skill of compulsory figures with the skater's creativity. In Vienna, Austria, in 1882, the first "international skating meeting" was held. In that first international competition, each contestant was required to perform twenty-three prescribed compulsory figures, plus one special pattern of his (competitions were all-male) own design, and a four-minute free-skating (artistic) routine. The first, second, and third winners of that competition were Leopold Frey (a student of Jackson Haines), Eduard Englemann of Austria, and Axel Paulsen of Norway. First prize was a statuette of Haines, skating's greatest innovator. These contests gained in popularity and quickly spread through Europe, attracting larger audiences and bigger prizes.

In the early years of competitive skating, rules governing the sport and its contests varied from country to country. As more competitions were staged, standardization of the sport became necessary. From this need developed national skating associations. The first governing body for skating was formed in Canada in 1878, followed by the National Skating Association of Great Britain a year later. The United States Figure Skating Association (USFSA) was not formed until 1921.

INTERNATIONAL SKATING UNION

Before the turn of the century, interest in figure skating grew rapidly. More and more competitions were held and the number of competitors swelled. An international association to govern and control figure skating became necessary to conduct competitions, train judges, and settle all international disputes. In 1892 representatives from the national skating associations of Great Britain, the Netherlands, Sweden, Germany, and Hungary met in Davos, Switzerland, and created the International Skating Union (ISU).

When the ISU was formed in 1892, its major concern was to establish control over both speed and artistic skating, to limit the prizes awarded in competition, and at the same time to define the rules concerning amateurs. One result of the formation of this new organization was the banning from ISU events of all but strictly amateur skaters. This ban excluded Axel Paulsen, the inventor of the Axel jump, who had received money in speed-skating races.

WORLD FIGURE SKATING CHAMPIONSHIPS

In 1896 the ISU organized and sanctioned the first World Figure Skating Championships, held in Leningrad (St. Petersburg), Russia. They have been held annually ever since—except for interruptions during both World Wars. In 1902, Mrs. Madge Syers Cave was the first woman to enter the world championships. When she won the silver medal, the ISU decided to hold separate competitions for men and women beginning in 1906. The competition in 1896 consisted of both compulsory figures and free skating. Today there are four events: men's singles, with three compulsory figures, a two-minute short program with compulsory moves, and a five-minute free-skating program; ladies' singles, the same as for the men except that the women skate a four-minute free-skating program; pairs skating, a two-minute short program with compulsory moves, and a five-minute free-skating program; and ice dancing, three compulsory dances, an original set-pattern dance, and a five-minute free dance. It is possible that the time will be shortened for men and women in the near future. The first women's event was in 1906, the pairs event began in 1908, and the ice dancing began in 1952.

The competitors in the world championships are selected by each member nation of the ISU. The governing body of each country is allowed to enter at least one contestant in each of the four events. If in the immediately preceding world championships a nation has had a competitor finish among the top ten placings, then that nation may enter two competitors in that event. If a nation has also had a competitor finish in the top five placings, then that skater and two others may be entered, but never more than three singles skaters, pair teams, or dance couples from one country may compete in one event. The skaters selected to compete by their national governing committees are usually, but not necessarily, the national champions plus one or two of a nation's best competitors.

The host of the annual world championships is determined by the ISU Council. Member nations and their governing bodies desiring to host a world championship submit their bids to the ISU. The ISU Council carefully considers each bid and makes a decision. The submitted bid is a detailed outline of the proposed site of the event, including the arena, hotels, travel arrangements, and projected costs and revenues.

The championships, held each year in March, rotate their locale; every third year the events are held in North America (1975, 1978, 1981, etc.).

ISU determines the maneuvers to be skated in international competitions, the lengths of speed-skating races, and the shapes of the courses. Two years before each European, World, and Olympic competition, the ISU Council, at its annual meetings, draws by lot the compulsory figures groups, the group of required elements for singles and pairs short programs, and the compulsory dances and the original set-pattern rhythm—foxtrot, tango, waltz, etc.—for ice dancing. This allows the skaters, coaches, and officials ample time to prepare for each season's competition.

In addition to the World and European championships, the ISU has established the "Junior" World Figure Skating Championship. It was first held in 1976 at Megève, France. This event has both age and experience restrictions. Singles skaters must not have reached their sixteenth birthday by July 1 of the preceding year, and neither partner of a pair or couple may have reached age eighteen by that same date. Entrants may neither have participated in a World or European championship or in the Olympics, nor have placed in the top three in a senior international event.

Recently the United States has adopted a policy of sending promising young skaters to gain valuable experience at many of the senior international skating events held each fall. Early exposure to international competition is essential for the skaters because it not only makes them better competitors, but it gives them a chance to represent their country in an international event. The skaters gain a great deal of composure and know-how from these events, and it also gives the international judges a chance to see the skaters develop. Funds for this purpose are drawn from the United States Figure Skating Association Memorial Fund, which was established in 1961 in memory of the United States World Figure Skating Team that was lost in an air crash on the way to the 1961 World Figure Skating Championships in Brussels.

EUROPEAN FIGURE SKATING CHAMPIONSHIPS

The European Figure Skating Championships were first held in Hamburg, Germany, in 1891. The event had seven competitors, five from Germany and two from Austria, and consisted of compulsory figures only. The competition moved to Vienna in 1892 and added "artistic" skating to the compulsory figures.

It was not until 1893 that the European Figure Skating Championships were recognized by the ISU. However, that recognition was short-lived, as the ISU Congress—its decision-making body—declared in 1895 that the European Championships of 1893 were "invalid." The events were suspended in 1896 and 1897 because the ISU conducted the World Figure Skating Championships and saw the European Championships as irrelevant. But by 1898 the ISU realized that both events could survive together and its sanction of the European Championships "revalidated" the results of the 1893 event.

The program of today's competition is the same as in the world championships. It consists of four events—men's and ladies' singles, pairs skating, and ice dancing. The singles each perform three compulsory figures, a short program, and a free-skating routine. Again, the pairs skate a short program and a free-skating routine, while the dancers present three compulsory dances, an original set-pattern dance, and a free dance.

The competitors in the European Championships are selected by each participating national governing body. Each European member of the ISU is allowed to enter at least one competitor in each event (one couple or pair, too) and, depending on the previous year's results, additional competitors.

Prior to 1948 the events were open to all members of European skating clubs. This meant that skaters from North America were eligible to compete if they belonged to a skating club in Europe. In 1948, the men's event was won by Dick Button of the United States, and the ladies' event was won by Barbara Ann Scott of Canada. The European Championships were then closed to all but European skaters. That same year, Button and Scott went on to win their respective national titles in addition to the World and Olympic titles.

Like the World Figure Skating Championships, the European events are held in a different city each year. National governing bodies wishing to host the events submit to the ISU bids detailing the proposed site and facilities. The competition is held each year in late January or the first week of February.

THE WINTER OLYMPICS

Figure skating is the oldest event of the Winter Olympic Games, becoming a part of the Olympic program in 1908. (The modern Olympics began in 1896 as a series of summer events.) Although figure skating became a part of the Olympic program in 1908, the winter games became a separate event in 1924. Since then, they have been held every four years, except between 1936 and 1948 because of World War II.

When the Olympic figure-skating event first began, it included men's singles, ladies' singles, and pairs skating. In 1976 ice dancing was added for the first time. Sonja Henie of Norway revolutionized figure skating for women when she wore a skating costume in the 1924 Olympics (instead of an ankle-length skirt) and performed jumps and spins in her free-skating program that had previously been performed only by men. Although she came in last in 1924 at age eleven, she went on to win ten World Championship titles and three consecutive Olympic gold medals.

The Olympics are scheduled for the second and third weeks in February, four weeks before the World Championships. According to ISU rules, the number of competitors from each country is determined by the placement of their skaters in the World Championships of the previous year. Each country may send two skaters; and those countries whose skaters placed in the top five at Worlds in the previous year may send three entrants to the Olympics.

The skating requirements for each category resemble those stated for the World Championships and the European Championships.

THE UNITED STATES NATIONALS

To compete in the United States Championships, a skater follows a specific progression. The nation is divided into three sections—Eastern, Midwestern, and Pacific Coast—which, in turn, are divided into three regions. Each of the nine geographic regions conducts its own championships known as subsectionals, sending its first, second, and third place medal winners on to sectional competitions. Finally, the medal winners of the three sectional competitions advance to the national championships and compete for the United States figure-skating title in each skating level—novice, junior, and senior. Medal winners in the senior or gold events represent the United States in Olympic and world competitions.

TESTS

A vital part of the USFSA is its series of proficiency tests. The USFSA Tests are constructed and designed to be a cumulation of steps in the progress of each skater. As of May 1, 1980, there are nine figure-skating tests, six free-skating tests, five pairs tests, and six dance tests. The tests are a progression, and a skater must fully master the skills required for one test before he or she is ready for the next test. However, the tests also provide encouragement for the skater, showing proof of skating skill. And it is the test level of a skater that determines what event(s) may be entered in competition.

The USFSA Tests are administered and sanctioned by rules established by the USFSA and enforced by member figure-skating clubs. Each USFSA club has a "test chairperson" whose responsibility includes the supervision of all tests taken within his or her club. Tests are usually given in one day, called a "test session." These sessions are announced well in advance and are held on days reserved exclusively for the taking and judging of tests. Sometimes there are specific days for figure- and free-skating tests that are separated from dance and pairs tests.

As skaters take a test, they are evaluated by a panel of judges—no fewer than three judges, and always an odd number—and their recorded marks are sent to the USFSA National Headquarters in Colorado Springs, Colorado, where all records are kept, ready for reference.

JUDGES

The judges are trained through experience, and just as there are different levels of skaters, there are different levels of judges. A good judge will recognize the various styles and techniques of skaters as they reflect the philosophies of coaches and "schools," but the primary concern should be the end result of that training—the performance itself. Judges evaluate accuracy, firmness of balance, fluidity, while assessing the program on composition, interpretation of the music, and the harmony of the style with the music.

Because a point system is used in scoring, judges necessarily split hairs during a competition. And often the difference between the champion and second place is just that, a hair's breadth. Coaches may influence a skater's style, but the standard of skating is set by the judges.

SOME THOUGHTS about COACHING

GOOD COACHING VERSUS GOOD TEACHING

I am going to make a distinction between a coach and a teacher. A teacher or instructor shows you how to do a figure or a particular skating movement. A coach, on the other hand, not only helps you to improve a figure but advises you about your diet, keeps your family away from you when they become bothersome, makes sure you have the right pair of skates, and sees that you get up at the right time for a competition.

Some people are excellent teachers—yet they may not be good coaches. To be effective, the instructor must know his or her craft and must be able to pass this along to you. To be a good coach requires much more than skating knowledge to prepare you for competition and to help you realize your potential. Even though all good teachers may not be good coaches, all good coaches are necessarily good teachers.

To train a champion, a coach must be willing to adapt and adjust his or her methods to each skater. That is the key to good coaching.

We are not all born with the same body, the same flexibility, or the same motivation, so what a coach has discovered as the "best technique" for one skater may not be the "best" for another. A coach who is rigid about his "best technique" will prevent the skater with good potential from developing his or her full capacity. On the other hand, when a coach shapes the technique to meet the needs of the skater, a champion may emerge.

The style of an athlete, regardless of the sport, is always dictated by physical characteristics. A skater with short legs will have a different style than a skater with long legs; one is not necessarily better than the other, only different. There are short skaters with excellent style and tall skaters with excellent style. But it is up to the coach to help each skater discover his or her own particular talents and develop them.

Another basic maxim for the coach is that the teaching method must be made easy to understand. The coach can eliminate many unnecessary obstacles by breaking down every move into its simplest terms so it can be learned quickly and painlessly.

Some teachers make the major mistake of lecturing to their students about muscle structure and torque and biophysics. While scientific jargon may impress the parents, it usually does not help the pupil. "Keep that shoulder down!" will mean much more to the student in practice than "Depress the clavicle!"

Another common coaching error is to compound a skater's mistakes by trying to correct too much at one time. Sometimes an error is the result of several factors, and when it is spotted it must be corrected step by step. The coach must determine the causes of the error and then correct the heart of the problem. Only by successfully tackling one obstacle at a time will the coach enable the overall performance of a skater to continue to develop.

A coach must have many qualities. Of these, I think I would rank patience and an intrinsic love for the students as most important. If the coach does not like a pupil, it will be sensed immediately, not only by the pupil but by the coach's other students as well. This will seriously hinder the pupil's progress. The coach, of course, must maintain discipline, but a mutual understanding and respect between skaters and coach is vital; the skaters must know the coach is totally behind them.

Too many coaches have big egos, which often gets in the way of a skater's development. The skater must know and feel that the coach is there for the skater's improvement, not for the coach's glorification. The skater does the skating and wins the competitions, so that is where the credit, and at times the blame too, should lie. If a skater does well it may reflect on the coach, but the skater is the one who gives the performance that is judged, not the coach. The good coach never makes the skater feel he or she is there to make the coach look good. Too many coaches have said, "He skated so poorly, look at what he has done to me!" The skater was not even thinking about the coach while on the ice. The skater only wants to do his or her best, and the coach's reaction is the farthest thing from a skater's mind during a competition. A skater, by a poor performance, has done nothing to the coach.

GETTING ALONG WITH PARENTS

The relationship between the parents and the coach varies from nation to nation. In some countries, particularly the Eastern-bloc nations, the skater is completely sponsored by the national skating association and the parents are absent from the skating scene—an ideal setting for the coach. However, in the United States the parents pay the bills and the coach must reckon with them. It is my experience that the majority of parents are understanding and try hard to do what is best for their children, but unfortunately they are almost never objective. Thus the parents must be dealt with diplomatically. The coach must tell the parents of the skater's ability and never raise false hopes or give empty encouragement. In some cases, parents must be told that they have overestimated their child's ability.

But parents can also be a tremendous help and motivation to skaters. In fact, without them, some skaters would never become champions. Without Mrs. Fleming, Peggy Fleming would never have become United States Olympic Champion in 1968.

In any event the parents must be admired. It is usually they who drive their children to the rink at five thirty in the morning and sit patiently on a cold bench, often with no coffee because the coffee shop does not open until eight. After freezing at the rink for an hour and a half, they take their kids to school, bringing them back to the rink at three thirty for more long hours of waiting. These parents deserve a lot of credit!

Since the parents cannot be objective about the skater, the coach must be, especially when criticized by either parents or judges. At times tempers will flare but the coach must always maintain equanimity and deal gently with anger if it comes his way. It is a good idea never to react immediately to a nasty letter from a parent. The criticism never looks so bad after a day's wait.

AT COMPETITIONS

Part of the job of a coach is always to be with his or her skaters at a competition. Even during a disastrous performance the coach must stay at the barrier to meet the students as they come off the ice. If the performance has been less than spectacular, this is not the time to detail the mistakes. The coach should greet the skater after with reassurance and support—win, lose, or draw. Later, when both coach and skater are calmer, the performance can be gone over step by step.

It is vital that the coach never appear nervous before a competition. Sometimes it is difficult not to be nervous, but anxious skaters will depend on their coach for comfort and strength. A nervous coach makes the skater feel his or her ability is in doubt. And a bad case of nerves is invariably passed along to the skater. This usually hurts the performance, so anything the coach can do to remain calm is desirable. (One preventive measure both the coach and competitor may take against nerves is a good night's sleep before a program.)

One of the problems a good coach faces is having two or more skaters competing against one another in the same competition. Here, more than ever, the coach must keep an open mind and be honest and supportive of each skater. The skaters must know that the coach wants each of them to do his or her best. The best skater will win. This is perhaps the most difficult part of coaching, but also one of the most rewarding. It is great to finish a competition with several skaters going "head-to-head" and not have a trace of hard feelings. It isn't easy but it feels good when it happens.

Good coaching is an art that may never be completely mastered. Good coaches continue to learn as they work with their students and develop with them. Good coaching stems from a love of the sport and its participants and an understanding of how to apply methods to each pupil.

GLOSSARY

Acrobatic skating   The use of gymnastics moves in skating.

Axel   A combination of the waltz and loop jumps, including one and one-half revolutions. Begun from a forward outside edge, the Axel is landed on the back outside edge of the opposite foot. Named for its inventor, Axel Paulsen.

Bracket   A compulsory figure, involving a turn that is executed in a manner opposite from the three-turn.

Compulsory figures (school figures)   A prescribed part of competitive figure skating, consisting of outlines traced by the skater on the ice. Each figure is made up of two or three circles that are tangent to each other and can be varied with different turns.

Counter   A compulsory figure of three circles, involving a turn from forward to backward (or vice versa) on the same edge, joining two circles.

Crossovers   A method of turning corners in which skaters cross one foot over the other.

Edges   The two sides of the skating blade, on either side of the grooved center. There is an inside edge, the edge on the inner side of the leg, and an outside edge, on the outer side of the leg.

Flip   A jump taken off from a back inside edge and landed on a back outside edge, with one in-air revolution.

Free foot, hip, knee, side, etc.   The foot a skater is not skating on at any one time is the free foot; everything on that side of the body is then called "free." *See also* skating foot.

Free skating (free style)   Skating moves including jumps, spins, steps, and other linking movements, which are choreographed and performed in competition to music of the skater's choice.

Hockey stop   A method of stopping very fast motion on ice; the skater throws both heels out to the right and makes a sharp, quick turn.

Long axis   An imaginary straight line that bisects the circles of a figure lengthwise. *See also* short axis.

Long program   A four- or five-minute competition program of free-skating components, with no set elements, choreographed to music. *See also* short program.

Loop   One of the figures, involving an additional teardrop-shaped rotation inside a circle.

Loop jump   A jump in which the skater takes off from a back outside edge, turns one revolution in the air, and lands on the same back outside edge.

Lutz   A toe jump similar to the flip, taken off from a backward outside edge. Named after its inventor.

Paragraph   One of the compulsory figures. Both circles are skated on the same foot from one initial pushoff.

Proficiency tests   A series of United States Figure Skating Association (USFSA) tests to measure the progress of the skater and determine what event(s) he may enter in a competition.